Manifesting
Mr Wonderful

First published by O Books, 2010
O Books is an imprint of John Hunt Publishing Ltd., The Bothy, Deershot Lodge, Park Lane, Ropley,
Hants, SO24 0BE, UK
office1@o-books.net
www.o-books.net

Distribution in:

UK and Europe
Orca Book Services
orders@orcabookservices.co.uk
Tel: 01202 665432 Fax: 01202 666219
Int. code (44)

USA and Canada
NBN
custserv@nbnbooks.com
Tel: 1 800 462 6420 Fax: 1 800 338 4550

Australia and New Zealand
Brumby Books
sales@brumbybooks.com.au
Tel: 61 3 9761 5535 Fax: 61 3 9761 7095

Far East (offices in Singapore, Thailand,
Hong Kong, Taiwan)
Pansing Distribution Pte Ltd
kemal@pansing.com
Tel: 65 6319 9939 Fax: 65 6462 5761

South Africa
Stephan Phillips (pty) Ltd
Email: orders@stephanphillips.com
Tel: 27 21 4489839 Telefax: 27 21 4479879

Text copyright Freya Eostre 2008

Design: Stuart Davies

ISBN: 978 1 84694 269 3

A CIP catalogue record for this book is available
from the British Library.

Printed by Digital Book Print

O Books operates a distinctive and ethical publishing philosophy in
all areas of its business, from its global network of authors to
production and worldwide distribution.

Manifesting
Mr Wonderful

Freya Eostre

BOOKS

Winchester, UK
Washington, USA

CONTENTS

Acknowledgements

I would like to thank all the amazing women who have been part of the Manifesting Mr Wonderful group: Sarah, Chris, Alison, Andrea, Emma, Sam, Tracey, Catharine and Anna. Thank you for believing in the *Manifesting Mr Wonderful* a long time before a publisher was in sight! Thank you for trusting the process and for sharing yours with me. I dedicate this book to you and all the other strong women who have inspired and supported me on my own Journey.

Thanks to V for putting me in touch with Carolyn and Carolyn for suggesting O Books… And thanks to John for saying yes!

Thanks to Mum, V, Alison and Emma for your feedback and encouragement.

And finally, thanks to all the men I have dated and loved, especially Howard, Regis, Matt and James. You gave me the motivation to heal my wounds and to learn to love myself. This book simply wouldn't have happened without you…

Introduction

A man has to find a good woman, and when he finds her, he has to win her love. Then he has to earn her respect. Then he has to cherish her trust. And then he has to, like, go on doing that for as long as they live ... A man is truly a man when he wins the love of a good woman, earns her respect and keeps her trust. Until you can do that, you're not a man.

Shantaram by Gregory David Roberts (An excerpt from a real conversation between two men)

Have you ever found yourself longing for *something more* when it comes to love? Would you jump at the chance to get involved in a relationship if you could only find a great one to be in? If your answer is 'yes', then this is the book for you.

Maybe you have been willing to accept Mr 'Good Enough For Now' because the idea of being able to rustle up *any* man to go out with sounds promising? Or perhaps you have been single for a while and have given up hope of ever meeting a decent man? Well all that is about to change! If you often feel like this, you will find the principles in this book will lead you to a place of greater optimism and give you all the tools you need to invite a truly fulfilling relationship into your life.

What if you are already in a relationship? Perhaps you feel your relationship (or man) could do with some fine tuning... or maybe you need some help figuring out whether you are with Mr 'Wonderful in Disguise' or Mr 'Thanks, But No Thanks'? Although this book is primarily for single women, if you are in the early stages of a relationship, or perhaps considering ending one, there are many tools in this book that can help you decide. You will discover how to accurately assess your relationship and what you need to do for yourself while you are working things out with your guy.

Whether you are Ms '*Oh My God You Can't Be Serious, Why Is This Happening To Me Again?!*' or simply Ms 'Just Started Looking'; if you are a woman who really wants to experience a wonderful relationship with a loving man, then you have picked up the right book.

♥ *The aim of 'Manifesting Mr Wonderful' is to enable you to manifest what you truly want in a love relationship.*

Chapter 1

Preparing

Setting the Scene

Just who is Mr Wonderful?

When I talk about *Mr Wonderful* rest assured, I am definitely not referring to Mr Perfect. He doesn't exist and more to the point nobody would really want him if he did. Relationships reflect our soul life and you would have a job developing your soul in a relationship with Mr Perfect – worse still, you would end up feeling really awful next to him which would defeat the whole object of the exercise! Finding a perfect man is definitely not what we are striving for here – I hope you are relieved to hear.

The term 'Mr Wonderful' came about when I realised that all the men I have gone out with, without exception, have made me feel unhappy. I recently realised my deepest desire is to feel *wonderful* in a relationship, not to just be in one for the sake of it. For me, feeling 'wonderful' means feeling comfortable, relaxed and loved for who I am rather than being in a constant state of anxiety, irritation or confusion, all common feelings in an unsatisfactory relationship.

When I was verbalising my 'want' in the form of an affirmation (more on this later), I kept using the term 'relationship' or 'partner' and it never quite felt quite right or specific enough. Then the penny dropped; if I want to feel wonderful then I need to manifest Mr 'Makes Me Feel Wonderful', which quickly became shortened to 'Mr Wonderful'. I have already started to associate this name with yummy feelings and this is *precisely* what manifesting is all about.

So as you see, 'Mr Wonderful' is simply a man who makes you feel good. You may decide to come up with your own name later in the process but for now, when you read 'Mr Wonderful' think of those warm fuzzy feelings that you want to have with the right man for you.

Manifesting Relationships

Recently I decided to have another go at manifesting a decent relationship. I had been single for about six months and felt the urge to meet someone with whom I could have the sort of relationship I would want to *stay* in. I started some manifesting magic and almost immediately a curious thing happened; as soon as I started to create a space for a man in my life (more about this later) I was overwhelmed with a sense that my ex was energetically in my flat, even in my bed!

This confused me because I thought that I was over him and this feeling made me question whether I was right to keep him out of my life. Although there are very strong feelings between us, whenever we had got together in the past, it ended up being a rollercoaster ride – intense but short lived. Intellectually, I did not want him back but emotionally, it seems there was still an attachment and some self doubt.

I got this awful feeling that somehow he *knew* because I kept bumping into him. Whenever I bumped into him, he usually casually offered to have another round on the rollercoaster. This time I was determined not to go there again because I knew what the outcome was going to be. Then suddenly, while all this was going on, out of the blue, I got asked out by another man in a very forward manner. The long and short of it was that this person turned out to have very similar energy to my ex and I was faced only a couple of weeks later with the same basic problem with a completely different guy – I had gone and manifested the same thing again!

The manifesting was working, but something was not right; *this was not what I asked for.*

Thankfully I didn't sleep with the new guy so I was able to move on much more easily. However, it made me ask; how do I change the kind of relationship I attract? It all felt so familiar and so predictable. *'How am I ever going to get past this block so I can manifest a decent relationship?'* I wondered.

Well, my prayer was answered. The *same day* that I realised that the new guy was the same deal, I stumbled across a manifesting book called *Excuse Me, Your Life is Waiting*. I read it from cover to cover in two days – glued to every page. Finally, the missing piece of the puzzle, the insight into what I had been doing wrong all this time! I discovered something important about manifesting that was causing me to keep attracting more of the same.

This is a very good example of how manifesting works. It shows how easily a new guy was manifested and how I was also able to manifest a vital piece of information to help me along on my quest. I was aware of what I was experiencing and much more able to let go of the new inappropriate guy than I had been in the past and believe me, it wasn't because he wasn't pushing all my buttons... au contraire! I believe that all the work I had put in up to that point gave me the resolution which allowed me to say 'no thanks'. I really did not want to invite another Mr Very Wrong into my life. It also meant I was open to receive the missing information about manifesting.

So, as you can see, I am not writing this book to brag about how easy this all is (though for some I am sure it is); I am writing because I personally have found it incredibly hard and I hope that you will benefit from my personal experience and research in this fascinating subject. I have tumbled down at many of pitfalls, banged my head many times on The Brick Wall and run blindly down dead end after dead end. (As you can probably tell, I am one very determined lady.) I sincerely hope all this means I can offer you a comprehensive guide that will accompany you on your journey to love.

Manifesting relationships can sometimes be a challenge because, by their very nature, relationships tap into the deepest and most protected parts of our soul. I have discovered that is it really *not* the same deal manifesting Mr Wonderful as it is manifesting a car parking space or a beautiful new dress. If it was, believe me, I would have been married years ago! Yes, the *basic principles* are exactly the same but the sneaky barriers that can block the manifestation of a loving relationship are far more complicated and deep-seated than that of manifesting a parking space. For some people, manifesting a wonderful relationship may be as easy, for the rest of us – especially those who have been wounded in some way – it takes a much more dedicated approach to get what we want and *really deserve* in love.

This book will take you through the process of manifesting Mr Wonderful but, more importantly, it will explore all those potential barriers to manifesting *what you want in love* so that you are much more likely to be successful in your quest. I am not offering you any guarantees or quick fixes, just the opportunity to grow as a person and enjoy the process of manifesting the love you want.

The Law of Attraction

Before we can go into the process of manifesting Mr Wonderful it is important that we cover some of the general principles on manifesting. First we will look at the 'Law of Attraction'. If you would like to do further research on manifesting then I have suggested several good books in the appendix.

What is Manifesting?

Manifesting is a word which describes the process of 'attracting' or 'drawing' something into your life. You could say 'creating' but actually they are subtly different processes. To create something suggests you are actually making it yourself, like a building a house, baking a cake or writing a song. When you manifest something you are asking for it to simply 'appear' in your life. Manifesting has a magical quality about it that reminds me of giving your wishes to the genie in the lamp. It requires a much more hands-off approach and a large dose of faith or trust in the Universe.

The difference between creating and manifesting is all in the approach. To manifest you need to first accept that we are co-creators with the Universe. As co-creators we can create things either through our hands (actions) or our mind (an act of intent). Manifesting is when we use our *mind* to bring something into being. If you want to create a painting you don't only sit down and think it into reality, you have to pick up the paintbrush. However you *can* manifest a painting by someone else without having to lift a finger.

Have you ever heard someone say 'when you are not looking for a relationship one will just turn up'? Well it is suffice to say that it is true in so far as you don't have to *make* a relationship happen. You don't need to 'go out and catch him'. In fact if you are *trying* to make a relationship happen, it will almost certainly have the opposite effect. In terms of manifesting relationships, it is important to really understand *what sort of action* is useful and what sort will push away the very thing you want.

So manifesting doesn't require the same kind of *action* as creating – it's a case of inviting things in. Now, here's the catch: we are inviting things into our lives through our thoughts *all the time*. The thing about manifesting is that you are doing it whether you are conscious of it or not, and whether you are manifesting what you truly want or not. *All the good and bad in you life is manifested*. This is because of the Universal Law of Attraction.

Simply put, if you think positively then you will invite and receive positively. Think negatively and you attract negatively. This is why 'positive thinking' is deemed as being essential for getting on in life. If you are indulging in 'negative thinking' you will end up manifesting negatively because you will be inviting lots of negative, unwanted stuff (people, events, illnesses, accidents etc) into your life.

You are the co-creator of your life *whether you want to be or not*. You may as well accept it and learn to co-create the sort of life you want. You are a magician and your mind is a powerful magic wand, so it will serve you well to learn how to use it rather than becoming a victim of your own magical instrument.

I use the word co-creator with a sincere intention. You do not need to believe in God, faeries or genies in order to be able to manifest your relationship with Mr Wonderful. But you do need to accept that there is something benevolent in the Universe that will act on your behalf. You *have* to be able to let go (of fear) to be able to manifest positively, so trusting something is absolutely essential. If you have difficulty 'letting go' then this becomes even more important. To make it seem less of a risk, you can always decide to put your faith in *the process* of positive manifesting or in the Law of Attraction.

Ultimately, you will reach a stage where you will be handing your desires over to something that will create and then bring to you what you have asked for. Whether you would like to call that something Magic, the Universe, the Law of Attraction, Higher Mind, the Creator, Source or God really doesn't matter. But you will need to consciously develop your trust in that something to be able to effectively turn your negatives into positives.

Learning to consciously manifest requires spiritual development, especially for those who have up until now been a victim of their powers of manifestation and have felt life is dealing them a blow. Nothing could be further from the truth; the Creator will deliver what you ask for, though not always in the package or time frame you have in mind. We are going to learn how to ask for what you want and that requires some kind of faith.

♥ The 12 Principles of the Law of Attraction:

1. The Law of Attraction works on an *energetic* level.
2. *Everything* is energy, including the body you inhabit. Your thoughts and especially *the feelings attached to them* are energy.
3. Energy vibrates at different levels and frequencies; positive = higher; negative = lower.
4. Energy is *always* attracted to other energy vibrating on the same frequency; like attracts like, positive attracts positive and negative attracts negative.
5. Your most frequent thoughts *and the feelings that are attached to them* will at some point manifest in physical reality: You are continually co-creating your own reality through your thoughts and *the feelings attached to them.*
6. If you are thinking *and feeling* positively, it automatically follows that you will attract positive manifestations into your life.
7. Thoughts with strong feelings attached to them are *extremely powerful energy vibrations* and our thoughts will manifest things which are a vibrational match; things that are vibrating on the same frequency (or level).

8. Our part in the co-creation of what comes into our life is in *sending out the thought/feeling energy*. The Universe responds by bringing us what we have 'asked' for through our choice of energy vibration. If we *ask* for positive by *sending out* positive then we will be *sent* positive in response.

9. When we are sent something *we can choose whether or not we want to receive* it.

10. Responding to something we don't want in a negative way will not make it go away. *It will make it stay or attract more of the same* because we are sending out more negative to the Universe, apparently asking for more negativity to be sent.

11. A conscious person can choose to *transform the negative 'don't want' into a positive 'do want'* and vibrate it back out to the Universe in order to change a manifestation.

12. You can change your life with the power of positive thoughts/feelings as long as you are *not too attached to a specific outcome*. Attachment is fear – fear is negative – and negativity will only attract more negative manifestations. Openness to what the Universe will deliver is therefore absolutely essential to positive manifestations.

If you have been in any doubt about how crucial positive thinking is, then I hope these principles have made it clear. Positive thinking is *not* about trying to put on a brave face or becoming more able to 'cope' with all the bad things that 'fate' has dealt you. It is vital that we find a way to see *our* co-created negative manifestations in a more positive light so we can respond with *positive feelings* and *attract something more positive* in its place. When you dwell on how bad (negative) something is you will only manifest more of the same or worse.

I have made it all sound really simple, which in essence it is, but that doesn't always make putting it into practice easy, especially when it comes to love and sexual relationships. We will be looking more closely at the process of manifesting but for now I suggest you copy these 12 Principles out and pin them up or read them on a daily basis.

Even if you are already familiar with them, this will serve as an important reminder about what to do when things are not going the way you want them to.

The Big Repellent

I mentioned earlier that there was a missing piece of information which I discovered had been holding me back in manifesting the kind of relationship I want. I am now going to share this with you.

As we have discussed, we are manifesting all of the time. The vibrational level of energy we send out into the Universe comes back to us in manifestations. We have touched on the fact that thoughts have energy and that feelings give those thoughts power. This piece of information is vital to developing the art of conscious manifesting because *nothing will keep us further from what we want than negative feelings.*

One way we can guarantee that we will repel what we want from our lives is by focusing on what we don't want or on the negative feelings that are attached to a 'don't want'. As you will discover, sometimes we are doing this even when we think we are being really clear and telling the Universe what we do want.

Knowing what you don't want is crucial. It is not that you shouldn't look at what you don't want; in fact, negative feelings will give you a very strong, clear signal when you are off course. If you get a manifestation of what you don't want, then you will feel something like anger, irritation, discomfort, fear or upset. This is perfectly natural and actually quite useful! Once you have identified the feeling and the 'don't want' then you can turn it around to see what you *do* want. Unfortunately this isn't always what happens when a 'don't want' manifests in your life, as you will see in this little story:

A woman meets a man at a friend's party and he asks her out for a drink and takes her number. He calls her and they arrange to meet in a bar in town. She arrives a few minutes late to discover he is not there. She takes a seat and decides he must have got stuck in traffic. A couple of minutes later she checks her phone – no message – 'Never mind,' she thinks. 'He will surely be here in a couple of minutes.'

Another five or so minutes pass and she is beginning to feel slightly uncomfortable sitting at a table with no drink because she had decided to wait to allow him buy one for her. She checks her phone again – still nothing. Now she is starting to get annoyed. 'Why hasn't he at least phoned to say he is running late?' Then she checks her diary – maybe she got the time or place wrong? She tries to reassure herself, 'It is only ten minutes. I should stop being paranoid! He'll be here any minute.' But the anger keeps creeping back in. She hates being made to wait – and 'What if he doesn't show up? How embarrassing would that be? How long should I wait? Should I call him?' By now her anger and anxiety is visible; 'What an inconsiderate man!' She mutters to herself.

A few minutes later, still not sure if she has a right to feel as angry as she does, she decides to buy herself a drink as it will give her something to do. She stands at the bar for another few minutes and just as she is ordering her drink he appears, all smiles, and he plants a kiss on her cheek. He is standing next to her and says 'Perfect timing! I'll have a pint of Stella please!!'

She is relieved to see him – at least he didn't stand her up – so she smiles back. She was caught off guard so she ends up paying for his drink. She feels disappointed; she thought he'd want to buy her drink – especially seeing as he is so late. He is smiling; he obviously thinks everything is fine. She catches a glimpse of the clock behind the bar – he is over 20 minutes late. 'Oh well,' she assures herself as she passes him his Stella. 'Maybe he just hasn't realised'

For some people time keeping is not particularly important. For some women, buying a man a drink is totally acceptable. Perhaps for some women this story would not even be worth reporting, such a woman would be relaxed about paying for his drink, at his suggestion, even when he was 20 minutes late. But for the woman in this story, this is definitely not what she wants. How do we know? We know because she was filled with negative feelings during her first date with this guy. She felt a high degree of anger, anxiety and self doubt because of his actions. If something makes you feel bad, it is because it isn't what you want.

Her anger with his lateness indicates that she doesn't want a man who is unreliable. And her disappointment when he asks her to buy him a drink tells us she doesn't want a man who won't pay for his date. If you turn this around it becomes clear from her feelings that what she really wants is a dependable, considerate man who demonstrates this by showing up on time, paying for her drinks and generally making sure she is comfortable and relaxed.

She can respond to this situation in several ways, but ultimately what we know is that this man is very unlikely to make her happy and if she continues to see him she is bound to end up experiencing negative feelings on a regular basis. She could decide to use this experience to help her to recognise what she wants so she can manifest something different. But watch what happens instead:

After they have finished their drinks he offers to buy the next round. Feeling increased relief from her earlier intense feelings, she agrees. They have an interesting chat about films they both like and she feels reassured because they have something in common and he is really amusing company. At the end of their evening, he walks her to her bus stop and says he will give her a call later in the week. She goes home feeling that the date went well, wondering if he will kiss her next time.

A friend calls her the next day to see how the date went; 'I really like him! He was a bit late and I ended up paying for the first round but it was all ok in the end and he said he will call! I think he likes me… and we have the same taste in films.'

It is now Friday and she hasn't heard from him since she saw him on Sunday. He said he'd call 'later in the week'. When does that mean? The weekend? She has kept Saturday night free (just in case) but she has an invitation to go out with friends which involves buying a ticket. She starts to feel anxious. Should she go with her friends or just stay in and watch a DVD if he doesn't call? Why hasn't he called? He said later in the week and now it is the weekend! Then she starts to feel the anger surge up again. The man doesn't seem to have any manners. 'He doesn't have to see me; it would just be nice to know if he plans to or not!'

The weekend comes and goes. (Her friends managed to talk her into buying the ticket – 'He can always see you another time'.) Then she gets a text on Tuesday at 7.30pm: 'Wot U up 2? Fancy a drink?' 'Wow!' she thinks. 'This man really knows how to annoy me!' Her initial reaction is one of utter indignation. 'Now he just expects me to drop everything and go out?! Arrrrrrgh...'

She may well decide to go out despite her anger, after all she did like hanging out with him. She may even have a good time once she gets there. But we know this man will never make her happy because *she is operating on a negative vibration when she is around him.* Would it surprise you to discover that she *always* attracts men like this? And that she usually agrees to go out with them until her anger finally takes over and she dumps them in despair and then has to take time to lick her wounds?

What she doesn't realise is that by *accepting what she doesn't want,* she will only ever continue to attract *more* of what she doesn't want. This is because she will be continually taken into a negative feeling state with men who behave like this and will be manifesting from the same low vibration. When she finally does get sick of this guy (because he lets her down one time too many), she will then angrily lament her bad luck with men. And she will tell the world, in anger, that she *doesn't* want a selfish pig, she wants 'a *considerate* man!'

In this moment she has finally recognised her want, which she has been largely sublimating. This discovery is good. What is *not* so good is that she is projecting it into the world *in anger,* which is a negative feeling. And, you guessed it – negative feelings are powerful attractors of negative manifestations. If she stays in this negative feeling while stating what she wants, *her vibration will remain the same and continue to attract negatively,* even though she believes that she is telling the Universe what she *really wants.*

Key points:
1. You lower your energy vibration when you accept what you *don't want* and
2. Telling the Universe what you *want* while in a negative feeling

state will only attract *more* of what you *don't want.*

This is because your anger (or other negative feeling) is actually associated with your *'don't want'*; you feel angry because you *don't want* yet another unreliable man. So you can see that you are actually projecting your *don't want* into the Universe if you project your *want* out in anger. And how many of us spend time lamenting about how awful our last date was when it didn't go the way we wanted?

The same is true of other more subtle feelings that can get attached to our wants which are actually really about our *'don't wants'*. Here is a list of some tricky feelings which can really serve to undermine a want:

- Pining or lamenting
- Worrying
- Needing
- Demanding

In a nutshell, all these feelings come from a belief that you must have something *in order to feel better*. This is a 'fix it' want - a *'don't want'* in disguise; you *don't want* to feel bad so you *want* something to help stop you feeling bad.

♥ *In order to get what you really want you must release your desire from any negative feeling vibrations.*

This is why manifesting wonderful relationships can be tricky for many of us. We can easily carry difficult feelings about being single, being in a relationship, men, sex, dating... any or all of the above! And to make things even more challenging, often these feelings are buried away or even completely unconscious. Our feelings can also be confusing or even sometimes contradictory. However, the one thing you can be sure of is that our feelings will be behind what we do and don't manifest in our relationships. The biggest repellent to getting our desires is negative feelings – that is, until we learn how to turn them to our advantage. That is exactly what we are going to learn to do in this book.

Key points about the Law of Attraction:

1. If something makes you feel bad, it is simply because *it isn't what you want.* This is completely personal, there is no point asking a friend what they think; instead, ask yourself *how it makes you feel.*

2. You will only serve to lower your energy vibration when you accept manifestations that reflect what you *don't want* and then spend precious energy fighting them.

3. Being in a negative feeling state when you are telling the Universe what you *want* will only attract *more* of what you *don't* want.

So it follows that to get what you want you must:

1. Release your wants from any negative feelings or attachments.

2. Raise your energy vibration by deciding to steadfastly decline any 'don't wants' that manifest in your life *without attaching negative feelings while you let them go.*

As you go through the process of raising your vibration you will almost certainly still attract some of what you don't want and so it is important how you respond. When you attract a dud date, indulging in negative feelings will only make it more likely that the next one will be the same. We will explore how to put this understanding of the Law of Attraction into practice once you are dating later in the book.

The Question of Fate

We have talked about who Mr Wonderful might be and covered some background information about manifesting and particularly on manifesting relationships. There is one more topic we need to cover before we can begin the process of manifesting Mr Wonderful: Fate

I know that some of you will be asking *what about fate?* Where does fate fit into the idea of manifesting Mr Wonderful? When people talk about fate they are generally seeing their lives set out in advance by something which they have no control of. When someone dies prematurely, apparently it is fate: 'When your time is up, your time is up!' Fate is also often attributed to lovers meeting, especially in spooky circumstances; when you meet that handsome stranger on the 9.15, because you missed your usual train, then it must have been fate!

People believe that fate is set in stone and therefore can't be changed. So it must follow that people who manifest don't believe in fate because we create our own destinies, right? To say that fate and manifesting are mutually exclusive to me is like saying that science and spirituality cannot co-exist, that you can't be both spiritual and scientific. Then again, many people would argue that as well! Life is much more subtle than that. All you have to do is open your mind and you will see how it works.

Fate, if it exists, cannot be set in stone. We have free will. We have choices. If we didn't then, from a spiritual point of view, there would be absolutely no point in us being here. We wouldn't have to think about anything – indeed it would be pointless even trying. Things would just turn out the way they were going to anyway. Fate, or destiny, is really not an excuse for refusing to take responsibility for your life and your choices. You *always* have a choice about what you do, where you go and who you get involved with. God would never say; this is your lot - like it or lump it. What sort of a God would that be? We are here to develop consciousness and you simply can't do that without free will.

♥ *Fate, or destiny, is experienced the moment when what you have been sending into the Universe comes home to you in a manifestation.*

The higher the improbability of an event, the stronger the sense of destiny there is. You *were* supposed to miss that train and meet Mr Handsome Stranger. You sent energy out for a handsome stranger (consciously or not) and this guy 'fit the bill' so the Universe had to conspire to get you two to meet. Because you both recognise the strong improbability of your meeting each other and the wonder of such a coincidence, at that moment it is easier to acknowledge that the

Universe must have had a hand in it. It feels really special and fated *because it was*. But you getting on that train at that time and meeting that man wasn't written in stone before you were born, the events were put into motion by yours truly.

There are many men that would 'fit the bill' of your desires at any given time. When you finally meet someone you can really love, it may feel like you have waited for your whole life to be with that specific man and that you had to get on that specific train to bump into him. In reality it was more a case of the Universe fulfilling your desires the most efficient way possible and somehow finding a way to deliver your manifestation to you. It just happened to be that man, but it didn't have to be. Remember that we are co-creators. Desire and free will is our part; delivery is the Universe's part. We don't know who or what will turn up, or how, but the Universe will bring you what you want and the moment of actualisation is destiny. It was meant to be *because you asked for it*.

There is another aspect to this whole 'fate' thing that we need to consider and that is past lives and soulmates. Soulmates can be positive or negative (learning) relationships. I have had at least two powerful soulmate relationships which tore me apart. I will never forget them. I believe that I have been in important relationships with both these men in previous lives and that I will possibly have relationships with them both again in future lives. These relationships are 'soulmate' because they stretch across time and the experience of being with them affects us on a very deep level. We agree to meet certain soulmates in a lifetime and so there is an element of pre-destiny, but we still have a choice (unless they are our parents, children or other members of our family) about whether we engage in the relationship and invite the person into our lives.

So fate or destiny does play a part in our lives, but we do have some control. We invite people and events into our lives and we can decide to let them go. That is our Divine right. The details are the part we can't dictate. You may love a particular man and want him more than anything. You could try manifesting a love relationship with him until you are blue in the face but attaching to a particular person or outcome with a person will not get you what you want. Being detached and non-specific *may* bring the one you desire but the outcome is not up to you. And ultimately it is not up to the Universe either – it's up to the other person! This is the other thing to consider when we are talking about manifesting relationships; there is another creative entity in the picture – your lover. Car parking spaces generally don't have a preference about which car parks on them. Your lover gets a say too.

Support on Your Journey

We are about to start the Journey of *Manifesting Mr Wonderful*. Remember, he is the man that makes you *feel* wonderful; the man who is perfect *for you*; the man who wants to be with you as much as you want to be with him. While you are raising your vibration you will be developing an inner strength which will develop your ability to hold out for the right person.

Manifesting Mr Wonderful can be lot of fun. However, as I have said, manifesting a relationship can also be very challenging for some individuals. This book will be challenging for many readers because it is *intended to deal with the blocks to getting the love you want* and these blocks often involve difficult feelings. It is impossible to do the manifesting without first removing the barriers. Some of the work we will be doing is profound and healing, therefore, it is likely to touch you on a deep emotional level.

♥ *The more challenged you feel with regards to creating the relationship you really desire, the deeper you will have to go on your journey.*

This is a journey that will require commitment, especially if you feel very blocked or wounded in your past relationships. The aim of this book is to guide, inspire and offer some support. However, for many readers working alone with a book won't be support enough. If you are serious about this, then I would suggest that you consider seeking other forms of support as you work through this process.

Of course, the process of *Manifesting Mr Wonderful* may be straight forward and 'pain free' for many readers but if you realise that you have issues that you need to deal with, or any part of the book brings up difficult feelings, then please do not hesitate in getting support. I will make suggestions for this where appropriate and there is an appendix at the end of the book with some useful resources.

I feel incredibly excited about sharing this journey with you and I wish you the very best on your quest.

Chapter 2

Assessing

Uncovering Your Inner Landscape

Why Assess?

Before we can do anything else, we need to assess where you are with regards to relationships. You need to know what inner landscape you are dealing with. The process of *Manifesting Mr Wonderful* is like designing and creating a garden. First you have to assess it; what sort of a garden do you currently have? What size is it? Is it flat, rocky, or sloping? Does it just need a bit of tweaking or will you need to start from scratch? Is it overgrown or barren? All these questions are essential in deciding how you will create the garden you want.

Once you have carefully assessed the garden, noticing its best features and the degree of work that needs to be done on it, then you can start the process of clearing. You will have to prepare your garden to grow the things you want in it by getting rid of the debris, weeds or other barriers that will get in the way. You may even have a dilapidated old shed that needs dismantling! This is the bit that will require dedication and motivation. You simply can't build a fantastic new garden without first clearing away the old stuff. The assessment will help you decide what needs doing.

If you try to by-pass the assessment or the clearing, you are highly unlikely to end up with the results you are hoping for. You may have to spend a considerable amount of time and effort on the clearing stage or you may be able to whiz over it – but either way it is important to allow the assessment to decide where you are rather than hazarding a guess. Once you have successfully cleared the way then you can get on with the fun of planting and finally tending your beautiful budding garden.

The Assessment

It is essential that you are honest with yourself when answering these questions. If you don't answer honestly you will only get stumped later and may have to go back. You deserve to be successful in your quest, so give this questionnaire your full attention. Record your first *instinctive* answer, the one that gives the closest fit, even if you don't feel it's a complete match.

If a question or the answers really do not apply to you, then do not answer it. For example, if you are currently in a relationship or not really looking for one there will be questions that you can't answer or wouldn't be appropriate to answer. This questionnaire is mainly designed for single women who are looking but if not you can adapt it slightly by not answering certain questions. It will not affect your scores.

This questionnaire aims to probe beneath the surface and may well bring up challenging feelings. Please make sure you do it at a time and place that is appropriate and read all of the feedback before coming to any final conclusions.

Answer the questions on a separate piece of paper turned sideways (landscape). Make a grid with 7 vertical columns and 12 horizontal rows (leave plenty of room for rows 8-12, as you may choose more than one answer). In the *first column* write the question numbers clearly and leave room for your answers. You will use the other 6 columns for scoring when you have completed the questionnaire.

NB: I use the word 'relationship' to imply a committed love relationship.

♥ ♥ ♥

For questions 1 - 7 choose ONE answer or write N/A if the question doesn't apply.

1. When you see a happy couple together who are obviously deeply in love, what are you most likely to feel?
a. Warm inside   b. Irritated   c. Jealous   d. Upset (sad etc)
e. Nothing particular

2. When were you last asked out on a date? (Not for sex.) If you have been in a long term relationship until recently write N/A.
a. + 2 years   b. 1 - 2 years   c. 6 months - 1 year   d. 1 - 6 months
e. Less than a month ago

3. Which best describes how you have generally been feeling during the last few months?
a.Content   b. Happy   c. Stressed   d. Depressed   e. Really mixed

4. If you are single, how long ago were you last involved in a meaningful relationship? (Do not include one night stands or a few dates.)
a. Less than 3 months   b. 3 months - 1 year   c. 1 - 2 years
d. 2 - 5 years   e. + 5 years

5. Which most accurately describes your current 'single situation'? (Write N/A if you are not currently looking for a relationship.)
a. I have been actively dating but nothing significant has happened yet.
b. I haven't met anyone I like enough to get involved with. (Though you may have had offers.)
c. I have been open to dating but no one has shown much of an interest (except maybe for sex), nor has anyone asked me out on a date for a while.
d. I have had sex but nothing more has come of it.
e. I have been getting over my last relationship or just not interested in

dating until recently.

6. Which statement most accurately describes what you think about the prospect of meeting Mr Wonderful?

a. I would like to think he is out there somewhere; I just haven't met him yet.

b. I am not sure if I can believe that anyone would genuinely be that interested in me or make me feel that happy.

c. I am really not convinced that my Mr Wonderful exists; I think I need to work on lowering my expectations.

d. I feel really excited and warm inside when I think about meeting him.

e. I thought I had met Mr Wonderful on more than one occasion; but they always turned into Mr Nightmare.

7. Which most accurately describes your relationship with your father during childhood and early adulthood?

a. Growing up I never really had a relationship with my father, or I don't remember him.

b. My father and I got on well to start with but then we fell out, were separated and/or drifted apart.

c. We usually got on well, spent time together and were able to communicate.

d. We got on ok but I don't really feel I knew him or could get close to him and/or I didn't really see much of him.

e. Either my father upset me a lot or our relationship was difficult and painful much of the time.

For the questions 8 - 12 record *all letters* of statements that apply. If none apply to you then write N/A

8. Which of the following statements apply to you?

a. I have had *more than one* destructive or very painful relationship with a man as an adult.

b. I have felt sexually violated on more than one occasion in an adult relationship I chose to be in (include 'non touch' offences).

c. I was abandoned and/or abused and/or bereaved as a child *and* my parents or care givers did not help me deal with it sufficiently at the time.

d. I grew up in a family where there was an addiction or mental illness.

e. My parents had a 'messy', split or emotionally distant relationship while I was growing up.

9. Which of the following statements are true for you at this time?

a. I can see a pattern in my relationships with men and I have made some head way in changing it.

b. I have had at least six consecutive therapeutic sessions and looked closely at my relationships with others. (Include couples therapy and/or working a 12 step programme.)

c. I keep a journal or other private practice to help me explore how I feel.

d. I have read at least three books on improving my relationships to myself and/or others *and* I do my best to apply what I learn.

e. I have at least two supportive female friends whom I can *and do* talk honestly to about how I feel.

10. Which of the following statements are true for you at this time?

a. I would never dream of allowing a man to pay for everything on a date, even if he was a millionaire.

b. I often sleep with a man within the first 3 dates.

c. I don't usually wait to be asked out; if I fancy someone I ask them out.

d. I would usually go ahead and call a man I had just started dating if I want to speak to him; I am just too impatient to wait and/or I don't see what the difference is who does the calling.

e. If a man I have just started dating doesn't call when he said he would, I am likely to contact him to check things are ok or to have a go at him.

11. Which of the following statements are true for you today?

a. When I get involved I often start wishing I was single again, or find myself wanting to back away, especially if he is nice to me.

b. I seem to be mostly interested in men who are hard to get or are unavailable to fully be with me.

c. I often attract or am attracted to men who seem to have little to offer or who are only interested in me sexually.

d. I long for someone to love but no one really seems to want to be with me.

e. I often attract or am attracted to men who treat me badly, or let me down.

12. Which of the following statements are true for you today?

a. I have had at least one 'successful' relationship as an adult. (It worked well but we either outgrew each other or decided to part because of circumstances.)

b. If I feel down or upset I know healthy ways to make myself feel better (not habitually using drink, drugs, food or sex) and don't usually stay that way for long.

c. I believe Mr Wonderful is definitely worth waiting for.

d. I know what it feels like to have a man treat me the way I want to be treated.

e. I have a full social/emotional life and would like someone special to share it with.

Assessment Feedback

Section 1: Readiness for a Relationship
Use the second column of your score sheet to record your scores for this section.

For questions 1 - 6, record and tally the total number of ♥s, ◊s and △s you score.

Q1	a. ♥	b. △	c. △	d. △	e. ◊
Q2	a. △	b. ◊	c. ◊	d. ♥	e. ♥
Q3	a. ♥	b. ♥	c. △	d. △	e. ◊
Q4	a. △	b. ♥	c. ◊	d. △	e. △
Q5	a. ♥	b. ◊	c. △	d. △	e. ◊
Q6	a. ♥	b. △	c. △	d. ♥	e. △

Max number of ♥s = 6
Max number of ◊s = 6
Max number of △s = 6

Scores

A. At least 4♥s and no more than 1△

B. Less than 4♥s and no more than 1△. (This includes scores of mainly ◊s.)

C. More than 1△

Feedback

A: Ready to date!

If you scored 4 - 6♥s and no more than 1△ you are in a positive position and are ready to date. You may already be dating and just want some help in attracting the right man for you. If you have been honest in your answers, it is unlikely that any major barriers are standing in your way. You are also unlikely to be massively out of practice or on the rebound. Check the rest of the feedback before your final prognosis, but it seems you only have tweaking to do and you will be meeting Mr Wonderful sooner rather than later – that is if you haven't already met him! If you got a △, then check what it is. If you can deal with it then you will be in an even stronger position.

B: Out of practice or lacking in confidence

If you scored less than 4♥s and no more than 1△ then you are either out of practice or lacking in confidence. You could be feeling ambivalent about the process of dating or getting involved in a relationship. There is some negativity standing in your way and you will need to find out what this is about. The rest of the assessment feedback will give you some valuable clues as to what needs to be addressed.

C. Possible barriers to dating

If you have scored 2 or more Δs then you are either very out of practice or there are some issues that will need to be addressed before you can proceed in meeting Mr Wonderful. If you only scored Δs on questions Q2 and Q4 then it is more likely that you are out of practice and will need to develop your confidence. If you scored 5 or 6 Δs then you have a lot of work to do which will take a serious commitment on your part. Only proceed when you feel you are ready to take the bull by the horns!

♥ **Statements that indicate a readiness and interest in having a relationship:**

- When I see a happy couple together I feel warm inside.
- The last time a man asked me out was either between less than a week to a month ago.
- The way I have been feeling during the last few months is best described as either content or happy.
- I was last involved in a relationship six months to a year ago.
- I have been actively dating but nothing significant has happened yet or
- I have been getting over my last relationship or just not interested in dating, but now I want to start dating.
- I would like to think 'Mr Wonderful' is out there somewhere; I just haven't met him yet or
- I feel really excited and warm inside when I think about meeting him.

◊ **Statements that indicate you may be sitting on the fence or feeling ambivalent about getting involved:**

- When I see a happy couple together who are obviously deeply in love I am most likely to feel nothing particular.
- The last time a man asked me out on a date was between one and two years ago.
- I have generally been feeling really mixed during the last few months.
- I was last involved in a meaningful relationship between one and two years ago.
- I haven't met anyone I like enough to get involved with (though I may have had offers).

Δ **Statements that indicate there are potential barriers to your being ready to date:**

- When I see a happy couple together who are obviously deeply in love, I am most likely to feel irritated, jealous or upset (sad etc).
- I have generally been feeling stressed or depressed during the last few months.
- I was last involved in a meaningful relationship two or more years ago or
- I was last in a serious relationship less than three months ago. (You may be on the rebound.)
- I have been open to dating but no one has shown much of an interest (except maybe for sex), nor has anyone asked me out on a date for a while.
- I have had sex but nothing has come of it.
- I am not sure if I can believe that anyone would genuinely be that interested in me or make me feel that happy.
- I am really not convinced that this Mr Wonderful exists; I think I need to work on lowering my expectations.
- I thought I had met Mr Wonderful on more than one occasion, but they always turn into Mr Nightmare.

Section 2: Self-Esteem

Score one point for each question if you gave any of the following answers.

Please note you may not have given any of them, in which case you score 0.

Q1 c or d
Q3 c or d
Q5 c or d
Q6 b or c or e
Q7 a or b or d or e

(Max score for this section is 5)

For the following questions score 1 point for *each letter* you ticked.

Q8 a, b, c, d, e
Q10 b
Q11 a, b, c, d, e

(Max score for this section is 11)

Max total score 16

Scores

A. 0 - 1
B. 2 - 3
C. 4 - 16

Feedback

A: High self-esteem

If you scored 0 to 1 then you have high self-esteem and are unlikely to have many problems in your relationships. Your high self-esteem will be a positive factor in creating the relationship of your dreams. This is great news! If you scored 1, take a closer look and see what this is about.

B: Some self-esteem issues

If you scored 2 or 3 then you are likely to have some self-esteem issues. You will need to carefully analyse your answers. To some extent it depends on which questions or statements you ticked. If you *only* ticked Q3 (c or d), Q6 (b) or Q10 (b) and *none* of the others, then this may not indicate low self-esteem. If you *only* ticked Q7 (a, b, d, and e) and/or any of the statements in Q8 and none of the others, then you are probably already working on your self-esteem issues. However, if you have ticked any of the statements in Q11 then you are *currently* suffering from low self-esteem.

C: Low self-esteem

If you scored 4+ then you have self-esteem issues which are highly likely to be interfering in your ability to manifest the relationship you deserve. The higher your score, the lower your self-esteem is. The level of your self-esteem will always be reflected in the relationships you manifest so it is crucial that you take steps to increase your self-esteem if you want better relationships. When you suffer from low self-esteem it is very difficult to let others love you because you do not love yourself fully. We will look at ways to develop healthy self-esteem later in the book, so don't despair! You don't need perfect self-esteem to start dating, but you *do need to be working on raising it.*

If you have only ticked Q7 (a, b, d, or e) and/or statements from Q8, *and none of the others,* then this score is likely to reflect past self-esteem issues that you have already been working on. However, if you have ticked any of the statements in Q11 then you are *currently* suffering from low self-esteem.

Δ Statements that potentially indicate low self-esteem in relationships:

- When I see a happy couple together I feel jealous or upset.
- I have generally been feeling stressed or depressed during the last few months.
- I have been open to dating but no one has shown much of an interest

(except maybe for sex), nor has anyone asked me out on a date for a while, or I have had sex but nothing ever comes of it.

- I am not sure if I can believe that anyone would genuinely be that interested in me or make me feel that happy or
- I am really not convinced that this Mr Wonderful exists; I think I need to work on lowering my expectations or
- I thought I had met Mr Wonderful on more than one occasion, but they always turn into Mr Nightmare.
- I often sleep with a man within the first 3 dates.
- When I get involved I often start wishing I was single again, or find myself wanting to back away, especially if he is nice to me.
- I seem to be interested in men who are hard to get or are unavailable to fully be with me.
- I attract men who seem to have little to offer or who are only interested in me sexually.
- I long for someone to love but no one really seems to want to be with me.
- I often attract or am attracted to men who treat me badly, or let me down.
- Growing up I never really had a relationship with my father, or I don't remember him or;
- My father and I got on well to start with but then we fell out, were separated and/or drifted apart or;
- We got on ok but I don't really feel I knew him or could get close to him and/or I didn't really see much of him or;
- Either my father upset me a lot, or our relationship was difficult and painful much of the time.

Section 3: Positive Outlook
Score 1 point for each letter ticked. (Max score 9)

Q1　a
Q3　a or b
Q6　a or d
Q9　d

Q12 a, b, c, d, e

Scores
  A. 7 - 9
  B. 2 - 6
  C. 0 - 1

Feedback

A: Positive outlook
If you scored 7 – 9 then your positive outlook will make manifesting much easier. If there are other areas that need working on then your positive outlook will be a valuable resource for you to draw upon. Keep building on it and coming to it – it is quite an asset to have!

B: A mixed outlook
If you scored 2 – 6 then you need to look at your answers to ascertain where the negativity is coming from, because there is definitely some lurking around. If you have scored low on self-esteem, that may be the cause of your negativity. If your self-esteem is good then it may be a lack of trust in men or the Universe that is affecting your positive outlook.

C: Negative outlook
If you scored 0 – 1 then your negative outlook is really hindering your ability to create the relationship you dream of. You are likely to also have low self-esteem, so you may find that your outlook improves as your self-esteem does. Either way, the book is packed full of useful strategies which will help you develop a more positive outlook.

♥ **Statements that indicate a positive outlook:**
- When I see a happy couple together I feel warm inside.
- I have generally been feeling content or happy during the last few months.

- I feel really excited and warm inside when I think about meeting Mr Wonderful or
- I would like to think that he is out there somewhere but I just haven't met him yet.
- I have read at least three books on improving my relationships to myself and/or others *and* I do my best to apply what I learn.
- I have had at least one successful relationship as an adult. (It worked well for a while but we outgrew each other or decided to part because of circumstances.)
- If I feel down or upset I know healthy ways to make myself feel better (not using drink, drugs, food or sex) and don't usually stay that way for long.
- I believe Mr Wonderful is definitely worth waiting for.
- I know what it feels like to have a man treat me the way I want to be treated.
- I have a full social and emotional life and would like someone special to share it with.

Section 4: Ability to be Intimate.

Score 1 point for each letter ticked. (Max score 15)

Q4   e
Q5   d
Q6   e
Q8   a, b, c, d, e
Q11   a, b, c, d, e

For question 12 score 1 point for each letter NOT ticked:

Q12   a, d

Scores

A.   Zero
B.   1 - 2
C.   3+

Feedback

A: Ability to be intimate

If you scored zero then you are unlikely to have any fear of intimacy getting in your way. This is great news and will mean that it will be easier to create the positive energy so you can go out there and get involved without secret fears undermining your efforts.

B: Some fear of intimacy

If you scored 1 or 2 then there is some underlying fear brought on either by a bad experience or a difficult childhood. Look to the details of the answers you ticked to help you decide how serious your fear is. It could be that you have already spent some time working on underlying issues, in which case you will be in a stronger position to alleviate your fears. Q4 and 5 are potentially symptomatic of fear of intimacy, but on their own, this is not necessarily the case. However, if you ticked *any* of the statements on Q11, particularly a, b, c or e, then there is definitely some fear about getting involved which will need to be dealt with. This book will give you many strategies that will help you but if you also score low in the 'self-awareness' section then you will probably need to seek additional support.

C: Fear of intimacy

If you scored 3+ then fear of intimacy is highly likely to be standing between you and the love you want. The higher your score, the greater the fear. If you have ticked any of the answers on Q8, this should give you a clue as to where the problem may be coming from. If you have been actively working on your issues, a high score can be a reflection of the past rather than the present. However, if you ticked any of the statements on Q11, particularly a, b, c or e, then there is definitely some present day fear of intimacy. This book will give you many strategies that will help you but if you also score low in the 'self-awareness' section then you may still need to seek additional support.

If you only ticked statements in Q8 and you have a high score in 'self-awareness' and 'positive outlook' then intimacy issues may no longer be relevant today, even if they have been in the past.

∆ Statements that indicate a potential fear of intimacy:
- I was last involved in a relationship more than five years ago.
- I have had sex (since my last relationship) but nothing ever comes of it.
- I thought I had met Mr Wonderful on more than one occasion; but they always turn into Mr Nightmare.
- I have had *more than one* destructive or very painful relationship with a man as an adult.
- I have felt sexually violated as an adult with a person I chose to be in a relationship with, on more than one occasion (including 'non touch' offences).
- I was abandoned and/or abused and/or bereaved as a child *and* my parents or care givers did not help me deal with it sufficiently at the time.
- I grew up in a family where there was an addiction or mental illness.
- My parents had a 'messy', split or emotionally distant relationship while I was growing up.
- When I get involved I often start wishing I was single again, or find myself wanting to back away if he is nice to me.
- I usually seem to be interested in men who are hard to get or are unavailable to fully be with me.
- I often attract men who seem to have little to offer or who are only interested in me sexually.
- I long for someone to love but no one really seems to want to be with me.
- I often attract or am attracted to men who treat me badly, or let me down.
- I do not believe that I have had a successful sexual relationship.
- I do not know what it feels like to have a man treat me the way I want to be treated.

Section 5: Receptivity towards men

Selected answers from the questionnaire are indicated below with a heart or triangle. Add up your ♥s and your Δs separately for all the following answers. Please be aware *you may not score any.*

Q1   a. ♥   b. Δ

Q2   c. ♥   d. ♥   e. ♥

Q6   b. Δ   c. Δ   d. ♥

Q10 a. Δ   c. Δ   d. Δ   e. Δ

Q11 a. Δ   b. Δ   c. Δ   e. Δ

Q12 a. ♥   d. ♥

Max number of ♥s = 7

Max number of Δs = 11

It is possible to score no ♥s and no Δs.

The ♥s denote openness to receive from a man and the Δs indicate a tendency to want to stay in control. It is impossible to truly receive and be in control at the same time, though we may vacillate from one to the other or receive in some ways and stay in control in others.

Scores

A. Two or more ♥s and no more than one Δ.

B. A mix of ♥s and Δs – including one of each.

C. Two or more Δs and no more than one ♥

D. No ♥s *and* no Δs

Feedback

A: Openness to receive from a man

If you have at least two ♥s and no more than one Δ then it is likely that you are able to easily receive from a man and to let go of control in a relationship. The more ♥s the better! This will really help Mr Wonderful find you and give to you. If you ticked a control statement, check to see where you are potentially putting men off giving to you. Sometimes modern women are unaware of how their behaviour is controlling rather than trusting of men. We will be looking at this in more depth later in the book.

B: Some control issues around men

If you scored a mixture of ♥s and Δs *including one of each*, then you have to look closely at your answers to work out what is going on. Obviously the more Δs the greater the need for you to be in control and the greater the numbers of ♥s the more happy you are to receive from a man. If your Δs came *solely* from Q10 then your control may not have come from having been hurt. It may be that like many modern women, you have a distrust of 'traditional' gender roles because they seem to put women in a powerless or subservient position. This could be an essentially intellectual issue for you rather than an emotional one, *but it still stems from distrust*. We will be addressing this potentially sticky feminist issue later in the book. If you scored any Δs on Q11 you definitely have trust issues that have come out of having been hurt in the past.

C: Staying in control

If you scored 2 or more Δs and no more than 1 ♥ then you are sitting on the control side of the fence and potentially putting Mr Wonderful off giving to you. This need to control comes from a lack of trust in men. You have good reason not to trust men because you have been hurt before. However, if you want a great relationship then you will have to learn how to distinguish trustworthy guys from the untrustworthy guys so you can become more open to receiving from men. The more Δs you scored the greater the hurt and the more work you will have to do to become ready to receive your Mr Wonderful.

D: Avoidance

What if you didn't score any ♥s *or* Δs? This is highly unlikely, but it is possible. The complete lack of ♥s actually says more about where you are than the lack of Δs. No ♥s at all suggests that you are not happy receiving love from a man. Perhaps you have not been involved with anyone for a while – or even at all? Either way I would re-check the 'control' list below carefully and make sure you are being honest with yourself. If you feel this score is indeed an accurate portrayal then I would read the feedback for B and emphasise it. There seems to be a lack of relationship experience which suggests avoidance, and avoidance is a subtle (and powerful) type of control.

♥ **Statements that indicate an openness to receive from a man:**
- When I see a happy couple together I feel warm inside.
- The last time I was asked out by a man was within the last six months.
- I feel really excited and warm inside when I think about meeting Mr Wonderful.
- I have had at least one successful relationship as an adult.
- I know what it feels like to have a man treat me the way I want to be treated.

Δ **Statements that indicate a tendency to need to stay in control:**
- When I see a happy couple together I feel irritated.
- I am not sure if I can believe that anyone would genuinely be that interested in me or make me feel that happy.
- I am really not convinced that this Mr Wonderful exists; I think I need to work on lowering my expectations.
- I would never dream of allowing a man to pay for everything on a date, even if he was a millionaire.
- I don't usually wait to be asked out; if I fancy someone I call them and ask them out – that's what women's liberation has enabled us to do.
- I would usually go ahead and call a man if I want to speak to him; it's not the dark ages. (Or I am just too impatient to wait and I don't see what the difference is who does the calling.)
- If a man I am dating doesn't call or show up when he said he would, I am likely to contact him to check things are still on or to have a go at him.

- When I get involved, I often start wishing I was single again, or find myself wanting to back away if he is nice to me.
- I seem to be interested in men who are hard to get or are unavailable to fully be with me.
- I attract men who seem to have little to offer or who are only interested in me sexually.
- I often attract or am attracted to men who treat me badly, or let me down.

Section 6: Self-Awareness

Add up your ♥s and Δs separately. Please be aware, *you may not score any.*

Q5   d. Δ

Q6   e. Δ

Q8   a. Δ   b. Δ

Q9   a. ♥   b. ♥   c. ♥   d. ♥   e. ♥

Q11 b. Δ   e.   Δ

Q12 b. ♥

Max number of ♥s = 6

Max number of Δs = 6

It is possible to score no ♥s or Δs

Scores

A. At least two ♥s and no more than one Δ.

B. A mix of Δs and ♥s (including a score of one *or* two of each.)

C. At least two Δs and no more than one ♥

D. No ♥s *and* no Δs.

Feedback

A: Highly developed self-awareness

If you have scored at least two ♥s and no more than one Δ then you have a highly developed self-awareness, even if you have struggled in relationships in the past. The more ♥s, the better your understanding is of yourself. You may have spent time getting to know yourself better because you have found life difficult and you want to find a way to change things. However, some people are naturally self exploring or were lucky to be able to develop self-awareness because of good parenting. Either way, this puts you in good stead to develop a healthy relationship with yourself and manifest the love you want.

B: Some self-awareness

If you have a mixture of ♥s and Δs, including one of each, then you are likely to still have some issues with unconscious patterns of behaviour that you need to explore. It is likely that you have made some headway, but you can still do more to get to know yourself. The higher your ♥ score, the more committed you are to changing yourself. The lower your ♥ score, the more you could benefit from developing your self awareness. If you only have one of each, the issues may not have felt serious enough to prompt you into doing much about it.

Self awareness is *essential* for good relationships with others and for attracting Mr Wonderful – especially if you have developed unhealthy relationship patterns. Make sure you are not missing out on Mr Wonderful because you don't want to look beneath the surface of your issues. If you are not ready to look yet, then it would be wise to wait before starting your next relationship.

C: Low self-awareness

If you have more than one Δ and not more than one ♥ then you are unlikely to have much self awareness and may be stuck in unconscious patterns in your relationships. You may know that things are not good in your relationships and you may even be aware that you struggle with low self-esteem but you have either not taken steps to develop your relationship with yourself or the steps you have taken have not been very far reaching. You may be able to talk to friends *or* have done some therapy *or* done some self searching on your own but you have not committed yourself to getting to the bottom of the issue.

The greater the number of Δs, the more you need to start some self searching if you want things to improve. The more methods you use, the greater your chance of success. Self awareness is *essential* for good relationships with others and for attracting Mr Wonderful – especially if you have developed self defeating relationship patterns. Make sure you are not missing out on Mr Wonderful because you don't want to look beneath the surface of your issues. If you are not yet ready to look within, then it would be a good idea to wait before starting your next relationship.

D: Emotional Avoidance

If you have scored no ♥s and no Δs then you are lacking in self-awareness and may also be avoiding getting involved in relationships altogether. Either that or you need to check your answers; are you being completely honest? If you ticked any of Q8 or Q11 then you will definitely need to take steps to get to know yourself better if you truly want a great relationship with Mr Wonderful. Developing an under-standing of your self and your emotional make up will help you get unstuck.

Δ Statements which indicate destructive patterns in relationships:

- I have had sex but nothing has come of it.
- I thought I had met Mr Wonderful on more than one occasion, but they always turn into Mr Nightmare.
- I have had *more than one* destructive or very painful relationship with a man as an adult.
- I have felt sexually violated on more than one occasion in a relationship I have chosen to be in as an adult (including 'non touch' offences).
- I seem to be interested in men who are hard to get or are unavailable to fully be with me.
- I often attract or are attracted to men who seem to have little to offer or who are only interested in me sexually.
- I often attract or am attracted to men who treat me badly, or let me down.

♥ **Statements which indicate self awareness:**

- I can see a pattern in my relationships with men and I have made some headway in changing it.
- I have had at least six consecutive therapeutic sessions and looked closely at my relationships with others. (Include couples therapy and working a 12 step programme.)
- I keep a regular journal or other private practice to help me explore how I feel.
- I have read at least three books on improving my relationships to myself and/or others *and* I do my best to apply what I learn.
- I have at least two supportive female friends whom I can *and do* talk honestly to about how I feel.
- If I feel down or upset I know healthy ways to make myself feel better (not habitually using drink, drugs, food or sex) and don't usually stay that way for long.

An Overview of the Assessment

The assessment is designed to help you decide where you today are in terms of:

1. Readiness for a relationship
2. Self-esteem
3. Positivity
4. Ability to be intimate
5. Ability to receive from a man
6. Self awareness

All six inner qualities are needed to manifest the wonderful love relationship you are looking for.

♥ *Manifesting Mr Wonderful is designed to help you develop these inner qualities.*

If you have scored high on all 6 inner qualities then very little is standing in the way of manifesting the kind of relationship you want, and this book should help you set things in motion quickly and easily. However, the vast majority of women who pick up this book will have at least *some* self-esteem, intimacy and/or control issues to deal with *and that is ok.* It is exactly what this book is designed to help you with!

♥ *Developing these inner qualities will help you remove the blocks to manifesting the love you want.*

Many of you will have already been working at developing these inner qualities and some may even feel dismayed that you didn't score as well as you might have hoped. Rest assured, this was a tough assessment and the work you have done so far really will put you in good stead, *even if you are still experiencing dating disasters.* If you scored low on self-esteem (as so many of us do) and high on self awareness, then congratulate yourself for the work you have already done!

♥ *You do not need perfect self-esteem to start dating but you do need to work on raising your self-esteem while you are dating.*

You may have picked up this book hoping for a bit of inspiration or simple direction only to discover that actually there are some challenging personal issues you need to address which you either didn't realise before, or you have kept locked away at the back of your mind. If this is the case for you – then please do not be put off! If you have little experience in developing these inner qualities up to now, then I hope this will be the beginning of a very special journey for you. If you really want the relationship of your dreams, this inward journey really is just the ticket.

♥ *Take this inward journey when the time is right for you. And once you start, remember that you can work entirely at your own pace...*

Chapter 3

Clearing

Raising Your Vibration

How Does Your Garden Grow?

Now you have assessed where you are with regards to relationships, you should have a pretty good idea of what needs to be worked on to 'clear your garden'. At this stage you may have to take some drastic action, or you may only need to make a few small adjustments. You may not need to 'start from scratch', but if you do, please do not despair. This is a very special journey – the journey to your self. You cannot expect to have a wonderful relationship with a man if you do not first have a wonderful relationship with yourself. And there really is nothing more rewarding or life changing than learning to love and cherish your own being.

In this section we will look at how to clear a space to invite the sort of relationship you want. Once you get going you may feel you want to start dating but I would at least wait until you have completed reading this book and made a clear plan – unless of course you have already started. Remember, there is no hurry; this is a process, so take your time getting your bearings before making or changing any commitments. If you feel you need to spend a significant amount of time on this stage you would do well to read through the rest of the book so the whole process is familiar to you, then if things naturally start to change you will know what to expect. May the Force be with you!

Understanding Self Love

Before we begin, we need to explore what self love is. In a nutshell, if you love yourself you are able to treat yourself with an unconditional positive regard and to take responsibility for meeting your adult needs. Loving the self is *unreservedly* giving to yourself what the best parent would joyfully give you. In fact, you could actually describe self love as 'self-parenting'. If you have little experience of positive parenting then learning this skill will be more challenging. However, it is possible to learn these skills from scratch in adulthood. We will discuss how to do this later in the chapter. If you have no good role models, then this will be like learning a skill such as reading or writing in adulthood – it will require determination and patience.

♥ 10 Self Loving Behaviours:

1. Know who you are (identity) and what is important to you (values)
2. Take your own needs and feelings into consideration when dealing with others
3. Believe you are deserving of the best treatment and respect from others
4. Know what your boundaries and limits are and how to protect them
5. Enjoy your own company as well as spending time with others
6. Make sure that you do things that make you happy and bring you pleasure
7. Take good care of your physical needs for sleep, food, relaxation and exercise
8. Only get emotionally involved with people who treat you well
9. Allow yourself to make mistakes and be imperfect
10. Accept others as they are without having to change them (because you take responsibility for your own needs and stay out of harmful relationships)

Having this special relationship with yourself in no way excludes you from loving others. On the contrary, it makes you *more available to fully love others* because you are coming from an integrated, whole self, and you will have so much more to give. You can tell yourself until you are blue in the face that you 'deserve better' in relationships but if you don't really know who you are or if you do not really like, respect or value yourself, you will be automatically operating on a lower vibration and attracting men whose low vibration matches yours. Learning to love yourself will make your life much more positive, will raise your vibration and enable you to attract more loving people into your life.

Without self love you are not available to have the loving exchange you desire because you wouldn't have a 'self' from which to relate. You have to start with a solid foundation – and that comes from deeply loving and knowing your authentic self. If you think it is selfish or pointless to learn to love yourself, then I suggest you start the process by *acting as if* you think learning to love yourself has a Divine Purpose. Perhaps the beauty and freedom of self love will sneak up on you and reveal itself when you are least expecting it.

By adulthood we have already established our level of self-esteem – our beliefs about our worth and identity. However, it is definitely possible to change how we relate to ourselves at this late stage without that mythical doting partner first coming to rescue us. It is essential that we take this journey of self discovery if we suffer low self-esteem and we want improved relationships. This journey isn't just a ticket to a loving relationships, it will also give you a magnificent freedom to become who you truly are. This will naturally improve *every* part of your life.

What stops us from loving the self?

Healthy parenting teaches children to love their core self. The loving parent's actions and attitudes become internalised so the child becomes able to take care of themselves and to develop equal adult relationships once they are no longer under the parent's protection and guidance. In an ideal situation, when children come of age they have established high self-esteem and a strong core self with which to go out into the world. This enables the young adult to protect themselves from harm and flourish as a productive, self-aware adult.

Unfortunately, many centuries of a deeply abusive hierarchical social structure has led us to an almost imperceptible (because it is so absolute) collective belief that we must work at becoming *less of a self* if we are to become acceptable to others and to a judgmental God. *Nothing could be further from the truth.* We absolutely need a self to function as a healthy adult. And you can't be centred in yourself if you don't know and love who you are. It is simply impossible.

Without high self-esteem and a strong core self we end up not only hurting ourselves but, just as often, we hurt those around us too. It is worth remembering that there isn't a bully, abuser or violent criminal alive who loves themselves. If they did, they wouldn't feel the need to hurt others in a tragic and distorted attempt to feel better. A society that is full of self loathing or depreciating individuals is a society that is full of suffering and pain. The best thing we can do about it is learn to self love and focus on raising our own vibration.

Rest assured; there is absolutely nothing indulgent about self love – on the contrary; *self love requires you to take responsibility for yourself and the life you are creating.* Self love requires a great deal from you if you were not taught as a child because you will have to seek out new resources and practice behaving in a way that feels unfamiliar and that often does not come easily. Self loathing is far more indulgent; if you don't like yourself then you have the perfect excuse not to take responsibility for your choices or change a thing because you can argue 'what's the point?' If you have difficulty loving your wonderful self, you are far from alone and it really does not have to stay that way. *Self love is a skill that can be learned* whatever your age and whatever your childhood experiences.

♥ *Let the first loving thing you do be to give self love a try.*

The Secrets of Self-Esteem
'Loving' the self is an action, not an opinion. Yet it is impossible to treat your self with care and respect if you do not have high self-esteem. So before we can really apply new self loving behaviours we have to develop our self-esteem. You should by now have some idea about the level of your self-esteem from the assessment. We will now explore exactly what self-esteem is and how we can develop it.

The term 'self-esteem' refers to how well you 'esteem' your self – i.e. how good you feel about 'you'. Every one *has* self-esteem; the question is whether it is high or low. If you have low self-esteem, then the negative feelings you have about yourself can end up affecting every aspect of your life because you cannot love yourself if you do not hold yourself in high esteem. If self love is the action, then self-esteem is the underlying feeling of worthiness that will determine *how well* we will love ourselves.

It is important not to confuse self-esteem with confidence. Confidence is about how well you can project yourself in the world. You can be confident and self assured externally, or about certain skills you may have; you can be perfectly able to put yourself 'out there' *even whilst suffering from crippling low self-esteem*. In fact, many people who suffer low self-esteem try very hard to cover up or compensate with a confident or successful exterior.

Equally, you can have high self-esteem and still be socially shy, quiet or lacking in self confidence in certain areas of your life. Self-esteem is basically a measure of how well you like yourself – how you feel about *who you are*; self confidence is more about what you feel you can do and how easily you can project yourself. Self-esteem is about how you feel about your *being*, whereas confidence is how you feel about your *doing*. The two do not always match in the same person.

People can feel that they have varying amounts of self-esteem in the different areas of their lives. For example; you can feel good about yourself at work but struggle with negative feelings about yourself when in an intimate relationship; you may feel great about yourself when with your close friends but have debilitating low self-esteem when it comes to your creativity. However, true self-esteem is not something that can easily fluctuate because of outside circumstances – *it lies at your core*. If our self-esteem seems to fluctuate according to what is going on in our lives, then we do not have a strong core self-esteem, and it becomes vulnerable to external influences.

What we are aiming for on this journey is to develop our *underlying core self* that is not dependent on 'how we are doing' in any area of our life: We are aiming to gradually transform our wobbly self-esteem into a *solid core self.*

It is a common misconception that self-esteem reflects 'how well you are doing' in life. Many books on self-esteem focus on developing your achievements and gaining merits or success. The idea is, the more successful you are in any area of your life, the higher your self-esteem will be. The solution given is to work on building up the areas you feel weakest and focus your attention on your 'strengths' so you can gradually raise your self-esteem along with your successes. You are also encouraged to re-frame 'failures' into 'opportunities for growth'. While this is a great approach for building confidence and success, it will not actually solve the problem of low self-esteem. If it did, then highly attractive, wealthy and successful people – those who have made it to the pinnacle of their chosen field – would never suffer from low self-esteem.

If anything, huge success and celebrity seems to *highlight* the pain of living with low self-esteem and can *add* to the sense of self alien-ation. It can lead 'stars' to eating disorders, addictions, relationship problems and even suicide. The media may lament that 'they had it all' and how sad it is that they 'threw it all away' but clearly, they didn't really 'have it all' or they wouldn't have been so unhappy. What was missing was a healthy self-esteem. In truth, no amount of success can cover up what we feel about ourselves: 'Having it all' externally has very little bearing on developing core self-esteem.

When this 'do better: feel better' thinking is applied to relationships (the area where so many of us come face to face with our underlying low self-esteem) we believe that all we have to do is 'have' that successful relationship and then we will feel ok about ourselves. And if a 'successful' relationship is defined by how 'loved' we are by the other person, then it must follow that, in order to raise our self-esteem, all we have to do is find someone to 'love' us. Thus, we find ourselves searching for the love that is given by someone else (external) so we can feel ok about who we are (internal).

If self-esteem could be found outside of ourselves, then this would make perfect sense – but it can't. Your core self-esteem can not be affected *either way* by what goes on outside of yourself. Once you are a fully-formed adult, your self-esteem cannot truly be raised or depleted *except from the inside*. As children we are supposed to look for external mirroring to find out who we are, that is our job. If we were wounded as children, we can get stuck and continue, like children, to look for mirrors that will reflect our essential goodness back to us. But once we are adults, we have already internalised the childhood mirrors, for good or bad, and *the only way we can change things is from the inside*.

This can seem unfair for those of us who received negative mirrors as children, but actually this is not as bad as it seems. Not only is there (thankfully) a way to heal your core self-esteem, but once you have it, it *can no longer be stripped away from you*. As an adult you *always* have control of your self-esteem, for good or bad. Ultimately, this is a much more empowering place to be in than needing the external positive mirroring like that of a developing child. When, like a child, you look for your self-esteem outside of yourself, it can be taken away as easily as it can be given, which leaves you powerless and vulnerable.

When we look to others to give us validation of our worth, even in love, we are giving our power away. Yes, 'achievements' and 'success' can help you to build your confidence, but they will not make you *sure of your worth as a human being*. This is just as well because what would happen if you failed at something or someone didn't like you, or your husband ran off with someone else? How can your intrinsic worth possibly be dependent on what other people do or say? Seeking external validation will only lead you further from yourself while building your self-esteem can only bring you closer.

The Big Black Hole

When we have low self-esteem we are carrying around a big, scary black hole inside of us that we know needs to be filled. The problem is that although the black hole threatens us on a deep level, as we have seen, it can never be filled from the outside.

When I was in my late teens I had a very painful relationship in which I was completely obsessed and focussed my boyfriend. I was so estranged from my core self that I had no alternative but to look to others to seek self-esteem and security. I honestly wasn't sure if I could live if we didn't stay together and that was an excruciatingly painful place to find myself in. We did break up and thankfully I survived, but only just. To this day I am not quite sure how I managed, and I did remain depressed for some time after. However, years later I found a place to sort out what I thought were my 'relationship' problems only to discover that I didn't actually have a self from which to relate to anyone else – *where my 'self' should have been was a terrifying black hole.*

I had been completely focused on others because I believed that if I 'got it right' or tried hard enough, I would somehow get them to love me back and then I would finally feel ok. I desperately needed to fill the black hole and I didn't realise that no one could ever fill it for me. Many people turn to drink, drugs or work – I turned to 'love' and often accepted sex because that was all that was offered. Of course, this only confirmed my unworthy feelings and further lowered my self-esteem.

All I knew was that I couldn't live with the black hole threatening to devour me. I had got myself into a deeply painful cycle with men because I knew love would save me but I had no idea how to actually get it. The more unloving relationships and sexual encounters I experienced, the more convinced I became that there was something deeply unlovable about me. The more unlovable I felt, the harder I tried to get them to love me because… *I believed my worth was something that had to be verified from outside of myself and yet I continually attracted people into my life who only confirmed my belief that I was worthless.*

To heal the black hole, I discovered that my two tasks were to learn what love is and then to find a way to get it for myself. In order to do this, I had to pick apart everything I had learned as a child about my worth and about what 'loving' someone actually means. In the past my need to be loved was so powerful that I would do almost anything to get the attention of the guy I was fixated on. I decided that if I put the same effort into healing myself as I put into trying to get men to love me, I'd be healed in no time at all!

♥ *Ultimately your true worth can only be found on the inside and experienced through your connection to the Source.*

Developing Core Self-Esteem

Self-esteem is intrinsically linked to our feelings of self worth. We are *meant* to think highly of ourselves, to hold ourselves in high esteem, to know that we are worthy of good things. When it comes to relationships, if we don't hold ourselves in high esteem then how can we expect anyone else to? Mr Wonderful is only able to treat you wonderfully because you *expect* to be held in high esteem, and because you already practice self love.

The difficulty is, when you have low self-esteem it is very difficult to practice self love (self parenting) because deep down you doubt that you are worth such consideration. Your job is to reverse this thinking by raising your self-esteem. There is a two pronged approach to this; you need to work on *both* raising your self-esteem *and* practising self love. Although you can start practising self love today, it *is essential to also work on raising your self-esteem by developing a strong core self.* This will make it easier to put self love into action.

♥ *Our soul purpose is to remember that we are Divine Beings worthy of love.*

Let's start at the beginning. For some reason you didn't graduate from your childhood with a healthy sense of self and your core self-esteem is a bit (or a lot) wobbly. You have decided that you want better relationships and you realise that you need to become stronger inside. You'd like your black hole, whatever the size, to be healed so you can be free to enjoy happy, fulfilling relationships with your self and others.

♥ *When you seek great love you are expressing the desire to become the empowered adult you were born to be.*

This desire to become empowered isn't only your birth right; *it is your Divine Purpose.* It is why you are on this planet having this life! The way that we create strong core self-esteem is by re-connecting to Source (God/Universal) Energy. This connection will enable you to start to experience your self as a Divine Being who is *worthy of love.* Not only is it really difficult to think badly of yourself when you are connected to the Source; but you will also automatically be raising your vibration and thus attracting differently.

♥ *Raising your self-esteem is the same thing as raising your energetic vibration.*

High self-esteem = belief in self worth = connection to Source = a high frequency vibration.

They are all one and the same. Therefore, low self-esteem = lack of self worth = disconnection from Source = a low frequency vibration.

So, in order to build self-esteem, we have to do the same thing as we need to do to raise our vibration; *we need to connect to Source Energy.*

Once we have a strong sense of the person we really are (a Divine Being worthy of love) and a strong connection to our Source, we can begin adding to our self-esteem through acts of self love. Your self-esteem will then continue to build as you become more successful at practising self love. So, let's learn how to re-connect with our core selves and Source Energy.

Connecting to Source Energy

The first step in building your self-esteem is to accept that creating more love in your life *is what you were born to do.* If you are following your desire to become more open to giving and receiving love, then you are right on track; you are following your Divine Purpose in life and that is indeed something to feel good about. And, whenever you have that desire to love and be loved you can remind yourself that you are indeed following your soul's desire.

The next step is to decide to stop looking for self-esteem from the outside and make a decision to look for the answer inside yourself. The answer to your worth, whether you are good or lovable enough, lies within you. It comes from an internal knowing and acceptance. Your true worth can *never be proved or disproved externally*; it can only be *experienced and embraced* or *rejected and denied*. The second you start to doubt your worth as a human being you are lowering your vibration. Believing in your worth requires the same process as believing in Source Energy (or God). It requires the same faith – the same *inner knowing* that is impervious to proof one way or the other.

The need for proof comes from wanting to relinquish doubt. There is nothing wrong with doubt, but when you apply it to self or Source you will end up vibrating on a very low level because *doubting automatically cuts your self off from Source (God) Energy*. You *have* to be connected to Source Energy to be able to experience it and doubting only cuts you off before you can know that it exists. (It can become catch 22 situation if you are not careful.) You can only have access to Source Energy when you say 'yes' I want it, I know it is there, and I deserve it *even if I have not yet experienced it*. When you say 'prove it to me first', you will remain disconnected and unable to benefit. It's really that simple.

So once you can say out loud 'I am worthy and deserving of love' (even when you have not yet received any proof from the Universe), you are ready to translate these affirming words into an internal *feeling experience*. Remember, you are no longer waiting for external experiences to make you feel loved or to confirm you are lovable, you are simply *accepting the feeling by opening yourself to receive Source Energy*.

When you are ready to connect to Source and raise your self-esteem, you can start 'the practice'.

♥ The Practice

Introduction

The aim of the practice is to become open to receiving Source Energy.

♥ *The practice is the single most important task in this book.*

• As we have discussed, low self-esteem blocks your ability to (fully) receive Source Energy. When you first start the practice you will begin dissolving any blocks that you may have. This part of the process may well take several sessions.

• The practice itself is very simple and effective, though your response(s) may be challenging or complex. You may find the practice really easy or very challenging or anything in between. It may even start out easy and become increasingly difficult as you get closer to your core self. Do not judge yourself or your responses to the practice.

• *It is essential that you practice regularly if you want it to work.*

• Firstly, you are aiming to dissolve any blocks so that you can become more open to receiving from Source. Then you are aiming for it to become second nature for you to open and re-connect to Source.

• Do not rush your process. If you have low self-esteem it may take some time to even feel a response during the exercise. Trust that your healing process will happen exactly as it should.

Preparation

Set aside *at least* one hour on your first attempt. Though you may not spend this long doing the practice, you may want to relax afterwards and gather your thoughts and you don't want to have to rush things. The first time you do the practice it is important to prepare for the possibility of an emotional reaction. Have something arranged for when you have finished – someone you can call, or a treat like a favourite film or hot bubble bath to enjoy. (Avoid using alcohol as part of your treat.) If you are someone who is prone to emotional distress, be sure to have some support available before you begin or maybe do the practice with a therapist's guidance. Once you have had a try, you will know what to expect and can allot as much time as you feel you need to do the practice.

When you practice, you can decide to do the steps in succession (one after the other), going as far as you feel comfortable each time, or you can do them in stages, focusing on one or two steps at a time. Although there is no 'right way' to do this, they are designed to be worked in chronological order and it is important not to skip any of the steps altogether. If you feel you have spent enough time on a step then you don't have to keep repeating it every time you practice, though steps one and two can really help build self-esteem over a period of time and are really worth persevering with.

Step 1

♥ *The first step is designed to allow any inner blocks to receiving Source Energy to gently surface and be released.*

Find a mirror in a private place where you will not be disturbed. (Have a hanky ready – you may need it!) Sit in front of the mirror and while looking at your self say *out loud* 'I am lovable'. Look yourself in the eyes as you repeat these powerful words for a few minutes. Notice and allow any feelings that arise.

If you have low self-esteem you are likely to feel some discomfort. However, you may not feel anything at all at first, especially if the 'block' is deeply buried. This is ok – it will come in its own time. The practice is a little like meditation in that you will find that your mind may have things to say about what you are doing. Just observe your response, whether it be in words or feelings, and stick at it.

If you find it particularly difficult speaking these words to your mirror image then try imagining that the person in the mirror is a friend and say 'you are lovable' to the mirror image, still allowing any feelings to surface. You can even try imagining that the person you are facing is a child who has been outcast or abandoned for many years and needs your love to bring her back from the brink… then find it in your heart to give yourself the same positive regard. (It is important to bring it back to the 'I' as soon as you feel comfortable enough.)

♥ *Ask God/Source/The Universe to hold you while you go through this process.*

The practice may be painful or bring up sad feelings, especially if you are feeling anything but lovable. Allow any tears to flow freely and be released as this will be very healing to your self. On the other hand, if you feel nothing at all, you need to be patient with yourself. *It may take a while, or several attempts to access any definite feeling responses to these powerful words.* Sit with it and keep repeating the words until it starts to feel like they are sinking in. You are not trying to force tears – you are just sitting with yourself and with whatever thoughts and feelings arise. If you do get an emotional response then try and sit with the feelings until they subside and you feel some relief.

♥ *Be there for yourself – she needs to hear this.*

(As I write this, I am suddenly reminded of the amazing film *Good Will Hunting* when his therapist keeps saying *'It's not your fault'* over and over to Will until he finally lets go of his defences, lets the words sink in and allows his sadness surface. If you are stuck then this is what you are aiming for but it may take several attempts. If you haven't already seen this film, maybe it's worth a watch.)

You may of course find the first step of the practice simply 'affirming'. If you naturally want to smile when you say 'I am lovable' (and it is not out of embarrassment or discomfort), then the chances are you don't have any blocks in believing you are lovable. Feeling good when you say the words is not the same as feeling 'nothing'. If you feel warm and smiley when you say these words, it is a sign that you already know that you are lovable and are ready to move on to the next step.

Just make sure you have repeated the words for several minutes and sat with yourself before deciding what your feeling response is.

Once you are able to fully experience *feeling lovable*, then you are ready to follow the next step. If you have had a big feeling reaction you may wish to stop here and come back to the beginning next time you do the practice. If you don't want to go any further at this stage don't worry; you need to feel ready and open. There is no hurry. You can do step one as many times as you like before moving on to step two.

Step 2
♥ *The second step is designed to deepen your practice and to continue removing blocks to receiving Source Energy.*

Repeat the same process in Step 1 for Step 2 and when you feel ready, change the words from 'I am lovable' to 'I am loved' and repeat them in the same way, using the mirror. If you are feeling unloved or have diffi-culty believing that you are loved then you may have more (or new) sad feelings which you can go with and release in your own time.

♥ *Ask God/Source/The Universe to hold you while you go through this process.*

Step 3
♥ *The third step will enable you to open to Source Energy and experience it flowing through your Being. You can either practice step 3 straight after steps one and two or when you feel you have completed working on the first two steps.*

When you are ready, the next stage is to consciously start to *allow the warm feeling of being loved to flood over you and/or through you.* This is how you open to Source Energy. Remember (or imagine) what *feeling* loved is like and allow yourself to experience it. Don't concern yourself with *who* is loving you; focus on the feeling experience of being loved as if you are being enveloped by a big loving blanket. *Feel* what being a worthy, loved human being is like and allow the experience to sink in. Smile at yourself in the mirror – even if it makes you cry or cringe at first, then once you have got hold of the good feeling, allow yourself to bask in it and enjoy yourself!

Once you are able to experience *the joy of feeling loved*, then you are ready to follow the next step. If you don't want to go any further at this stage don't worry; you need to feel ready and open. There is no hurry.

Step 4

♥ *The final step is to expand the flow of the 'Love Energy' you have started to generate in your heart.*

Once you can feel the Love Energy, allow it to expand your heart and chest area. Feel your heart being activated, pulsing with love and connection to Source. Then affirm to your self in the mirror 'I am Love'. If you like you can imagine the Love Energy taking the form of a colour as it flows through and around your body, while repeating 'I am Love' for several minutes.

♥ *Congratulations! When you open up and re-connected to Source Energy you re-connect with who you really are and where you really come from.*

♥ *Stay in this place for as long as you want and come here as often as you want.*

♥ ♥ ♥

If you experience sadness or pain at any time during your practice be assured that you are in the process of *dissolving the block* which keeps you separate from Source.

♥ *Ask God/Source to hold you while you go through this process.*

If you regularly repeat the practice, eventually you will feel only intense joy or perhaps even tears of recognition when you see your Divine Self in the mirror. And once the block starts to dissolve you will be opening to allow Source Energy to reach your core self and to start to fill the black hole.

This practice of allowing yourself to *experience the feeling* of being lovable is absolutely *essential*. Feelings are very powerful energy vibrations, so when you practice feeling loved you are building your self-esteem and automatically raising your vibration. You don't have to *think* about anything – all you have to do is give yourself permission to feel the warm energy flowing through your Being.

Smiling really helps. Caress or hold yourself. Allow yourself to get excited. Go with the flow and experiment with whatever makes you feel good. You may have a surge of sexual energy – and if you do, feel free to go with it, it's all part of the Source Energy and it is incredibly powerful and transformative. (But remember this is your own personal experience with Source – not about connecting sexually to other people.)

♥ *The practice allows you to experience being a child of God and you start to remember on an energetic level the bliss of being connected to Source.*

You are in effect becoming your own 'divine lover'. The feeling we have when we fall in love is exactly the same as this – which is why we often crave it when it is missing. You don't need to fall in love with another person – you can access this feeling by yourself directly from Source. And when you do meet Mr Wonderful, you will know that it is not he who provides this feeling – it comes from Source. He is a channel, as are you. If we connect with Source and ourselves first, then we are less likely to become dependent on receiving love from any one individual. This puts us in an infinitely stronger position because we can access Source Energy (love) without having to get it from anyone else. It is, of course, wonderful to experience love through another human being, but once we are adults it is no longer essential to our self-esteem.

Remember; the practice of connecting to Source is something that needs to be repeated often. It is definitely not a one time exercise; initially I would aim to do it *at least* once a day. There is no more powerful way to connect to Source Energy, raise your vibration and build your self-esteem than directly through your feelings. It may feel awkward, strange or even embarrassing at first. If you feel this way, then take it as an indication of how much you need to practice!

You are aiming to be able to access these wonderful, affirming feelings at will – anytime and anywhere. You want to be able to connect to Source while sitting on the bus or standing in a queue, not just when you are at home alone. Eventually you will not need to sit in front of a mirror saying affirming words to yourself every time you connect to Source Energy. However, these internal blocks can be very deep-seated and are often multi-layered, so it is worth 'checking in' with steps one and two every now and then, even when you think you have completed them.

The more frequently and easily you can re-connect to yourself and to Source, the faster you will see your self-esteem building and your raised vibration attracting more positive experiences. However, it is important to be patient with yourself while you are learning this new skill, and to remember there really is no right or wrong way. You will soon find that it creates such a good feeling that you want to indulge as often as you remember. Eventually you'll do it automatically when you notice something beautiful or inspiring or experience – something that feels life affirming.

♥ *Things will start to look very different once you remember that you are a Divine Being who can connect to Source at will.*

Dealing with External Mirrors
Once you have experienced a connection to Source and have begun to allow yourself to *know* that you are worthy of love, you can begin the next phase of building a solid core self. The secret to maintaining a

solid core self when you are out in the world is being able to discern which external 'mirrors' you choose to accept and which you choose to decline.

♥ *A 'mirror' is any external experience that we see as reflecting some truth about ourselves.*

People act as mirrors for each other all the time, but other events can also be experienced as a mirror. Sometimes it is something someone says, or the way they behave toward us but it can also be an impersonal event that happens to us. A negative mirror may leave you feeling that life is out to 'get you', like when there are no parking spaces available when you are late, or when you didn't get that job you really wanted. Positive mirrors are what we are all hoping to receive, such as a date from someone we fancy, a promotion or a 'welcome home' party. We constantly find meaning in what we experience, and we see these mirrors as reflections of *who we are* and therefore we can take it very personally. Most of us believe these experiences mirror our worth as human beings on some level.

♥ *It is crucial to have skill in knowing how to deal with mirrors if we are to create a solid core self.*

While self-esteem begins on the inside, you do also need to know how to respond to external circumstances and other people. Otherwise, you will find yourself responding habitually to negative mirrors and undoing all your good work. So the next step in developing a solid core self is to empower yourself to *choose* which external mirrors you accept. You can only do this once you know that *your worth cannot be found outside of yourself.*

If you believe that your worth can only be found reflected in others, then you are externalising it. When you look outside of yourself for validation, you are giving the power to the mirrors themselves, as if they get to decide what you are worth. What happens when the mirror you are interacting with is vibrating on a low level? Does that mean you have less worth? Of course not! Externalising your self worth will not only disempower you and disconnect you from Source but it will also make it impossible to have a choice over which mirrors you accept and which you decline because you are giving the power to decide your worth to the mirrors themselves. The time has come to take back your power. Own your worth and *give yourself a choice* about how you respond to mirrors.

As a child, you *had* no choice – you had to accept the mirrors that were put in front of you – however twisted, unloving or wrong. However, as adults we can choose not to internalise negative mirrors. This becomes possible when we realise the following:

♥ *Your worth is a given. Everyone, without exception, is intrinsically lovable and worthy. (However, not everyone is vibrating on a positive level.)*

♥ *The purpose of mirrors is to let you know what level you are vibrating on, not for you to measure your intrinsic worth.*

♥ *Negative (unloving) mirrors are there to let you know that you are off course and to encourage you to raise your vibration by reconnecting with your true self and Source.*

♥ *Positive (loving) mirrors enable you to experience yourself as the Divine Being that you truly are and to encourage you to share your joyous love with others.*

♥ *When we choose to internalise an unloving mirror, this only ever reflects that we have forgotten who we truly are.*

♥ *Only a loving mirror can reflect who you truly are, because we are all Divine Beings. Therefore, we need only ever to accept positive, loving mirrors.*

♥ *We need only ever allow a negative mirror to remind us to re-connect with who we really are through Source Energy.*

We will always come across the occasional negative mirror because we are not perfect, we are after all human. The goal, therefore, is not to create a life free of negative mirrors, it is to *become more conscious and in control of how we respond to them*. We *do* have a choice about whether or not we judge our worth according to a negative, unloving mirror. After you have created a connection to both your self and the Source your next step is to make a decision to view *all* mirrors that come your way as merely reflecting the vibrational level you are tuned into.

While you can't change the actual mirror from negative to positive (you are powerless over others), there are two things you can do: You can actively encourage positive mirrors into your life by raising your vibration and you can choose to decline any negative mirrors that come your way.

Declining Negative Mirrors

Once you have accepted that a negative mirror is merely a vibrational reflection, rather than a measure of your worth, it becomes easier decline it. To decline a negative mirror, all you need to do is recognise that you have stumbled across a 'don't want' and find the self-esteem to say 'no thanks'.

♥ *If a mirror makes you feel bad, it is merely a 'don't want', not a reflection of your worth.*

Let's go back to the story at the beginning of the book about the woman who goes on a date with an unreliable man. He keeps her waiting for twenty minutes on their first date and then doesn't contact her when he said he would and then texts her at the last minute for the next date. Her negative feelings in the story show she was experiencing a 'negative mirror' from her date. There are two ways to respond to this according to how high your self-esteem is.

A woman with low self-esteem will interpret his lack of consideration as further (painful) proof of her worthlessness, whether she is aware of this or not. She is looking for validation from outside herself and his treatment of her will cause her to feel bad and to want to feel better again. The logic is, of course, that, as he has the power to take her self-esteem away, he must have the power to further withhold it or to give it back. She is measuring her worth by how much he likes her so she starts looking for signs that he does like her, so she in turn can like herself. If there aren't any obvious signs, then she will focus on trying to *make* him like her by, for example, agreeing to buy him a drink rather than asking why he was late.

As she continues to externalise her self-esteem and feels more vulnerable, she will become increasingly focused on how much he 'likes' her. Nothing else matters to her because deep down she is not sure if she is worth liking and his negative mirroring has triggered a 'self-esteem wobble'. She will be desperately looking out for evidence of any positive mirrors so that she can feel better again and there is usually *something* to latch on to; he turned up, bought her second drink, walked her to the bus stop, said he'd call, and asked her out again. Meanwhile, she will also carefully screen out (deny or minimise) the negative mirrors; he was twenty minutes late, prompts her to buy him a drink, doesn't call when he said he would, leaves it to the last minute to ask her out again *because her wobbly self-esteem can't take the truth.* By screening out the negative mirrors and focusing on the evidence that he likes her, *she is counting on him to eventually give her back the self-worth she has handed to him on a plate.*

Although she is desperately trying to screen out the negative, what she is actually doing is energetically accepting it, *just by engaging with him.* She is not being 'positive' about him – she is being self-depreciating by ignoring what's really going on. She is choosing to internalise the negative mirror he is holding up. He doesn't really hold the key to her worth but she believes that he does. Because she is looking for self-worth outside of herself, this makes it very hard to let go. In reality, all his negative mirror reflects is her low self-esteem and how disconnected from Source she is – nothing more, nothing less.

A woman with high self-esteem, on the other hand, would access her worth and be able to act in a self loving (affirming) way: she would simply disengage and walk away. In real terms, she would wait a reasonable amount of time and expect him to explain why he was late. And if he didn't show up within that time, she would leave and allow him to get back to her about why he wasn't there. If he wasn't apologetic and didn't have a good reason she wouldn't give him the pleasure of her company again. She certainly would not have hung around after he had coolly strolled in asking for a drink, without even acknowledging his lateness. At this point she would have just picked up her coat and said 'I have to go.'

A woman with a strong core self would be able to know when and how to draw the line because *she would be paying attention to her feelings (internal) rather than looking to him (external) for validation of her worth.* His being late would not wobble her self-esteem thereby forcing her to hang around to find a way to claim it back from him. S*he would never dream of giving him such extraordinary power over her.* She would acknowledge her feelings, realise he is not a positive mirror for her, recognise the situation/relationship as being a 'don't want' and would simply say 'no thanks.' *She would decline his negative mirror.*

So, how do we get from being the woman who so easily forgets herself (and finds herself waiting hopefully for unreliable men) to a woman who has a healthy sense of self and knows how to take good care of herself?

♥ How to Deal With Negative Mirrors:

1. Build a solid foundation by practising connecting to Source on a daily basis.
2. Practice recognising and trusting our feelings when interacting with others.
3. Choose to acknowledge negative mirrors.
4. Emotionally detach from the negative mirror.
5. Energetically disengage from the situation/relationship.
6. Raise your vibration by reaffirming what you *do* want and showing gratitude for what you already have.

1. Build a solid foundation by practising connecting to Source on a daily basis

This will keep you emotionally strong and remind you of who you really are – a Divine Being worthy of love. *This is essential for your progress.*

2. Practice recognising and trusting your feelings when interacting with others

- Pay attention to your emotional reaction to others and identify the feeling(s). Are you feeling joy, sadness, fear, love or anger around that person?
- When you are having an emotional reaction to a person or situation, practice naming the feeling *to yourself.* 'I feel comfortable when I am with him'. 'He makes me feel anxious'.
- Also pay attention to other people's energy vibrations and listen to any gut reactions about them. If you are not sure, remain detached and observe while you check things out.

3. Choose to acknowledge negative mirrors

Once we have identified a negative feeling or vibration coming from someone else, we stop to check if we are being presented with a 'don't want' from the Universe. This isn't always instantly clear, but we decide to pay attention while we check it out. Once we recognise a negative mirror, then *we must acknowledge and accept this.* We decide to bravely face the truth, even if it is the last thing we *want* to know. We only injure ourselves when we go into denial and continue to engage with a mirror we know to be negative. We must learn to be honest with ourselves by accepting the truth if we are going to raise our vibration. We will get better and faster at recognising a negative mirror the more we practice.

4. Emotionally detach from the negative mirror

Once we have acknowledged and accepted that we are faced with something that we *don't* want, the next step is to let it go, to detach from it. If we are feeling detached in the first place we won't have much difficulty letting go at this point, even if we feel some disappointment. A problem can occur at this stage if we have already attached ourselves to the outcome with this particular mirror because of our low self-esteem. The best thing you can do to avoid this happening is to deal with your underlying low self-esteem by following step 1. When it comes to dating, it is crucial that you protect yourself from getting overly attached to a man before you know what sort of a mirror he is presenting you with. We will discuss this in more detail throughout the book.

5. Energetically disengage from the situation/relationship.

Once you have detached *internally*, you need to disengage *externally*. This means you decline; you say 'no thanks' and if appropriate, walk away. Sometimes it means all you do is walk away without saying a word or just don't respond. You *never* have to apologise, explain, justify, attack, push away, storm off, make a scene, argue or whatever. This step is most certainly not about creating a drama or trying to get the mirror to change into something that will fit you better. It is about *energetically disengaging* and you can only do that by saying 'no thanks', by walking away or by just not responding. Trusting yourself and your decision will make this step easier, as will practice. If you have never done this before it may feel strange or even deeply scary, but believe me, being able to walk away from that which you don't want, without guilt, shame, resentment or regret is truly liberating once you get the hang of it!

6. Raise your vibration by reaffirming what you do want and by showing gratitude for what you already have.

Demonstrating gratitude for what you already have in your life is a powerful way to connect with Source (more about this in the last chapter). Focus on what makes you happy and what you already have that is good. It is important at this stage that you connect with the positive – both what you already have and what you are aiming for. It is crucial that after saying 'no thanks' you then *follow up by affirming to the Universe what it is you do want.* Focus on your process of manifesting rather than focusing on what you have just walked away from – become wonderfully blasé about that! Don't allow yourself to be tempted to start thrashing it all out in your head or with friends. If you have any residual feelings express them and *move on.*

♥ *Focusing your energy on what makes you feel good and thankful always shifts your vibration up a notch or two.*

Changing the Way You Relate to Mirrors

You can learn to disengage from negative mirrors in *all* areas of your life. Obviously, the more entangled your life already is with a negative mirror; the more careful you will have to be about how and when you 'disengage'. If you are married to or working with someone who is acting as a negative mirror, this process may take some time and lots of working out. Sometimes you can't avoid a negative mirror without drastically changing your life. However, the principle is always exactly the same: You work at raising your self-esteem first, then, as you become gradually more and more detached from the person or situation, your energy can be channelled toward more positive, vibration raising thoughts and behaviours. Getting into 'the drama' with people will only serve to keep you vibrating on a low level.

This becomes possible when you know that the mirror reflects your current or recent energy vibration, not your worth. You can start to 'disengage' from someone *energetically* even if you can't (yet) *physically* walk away. The trick is, of course, to avoid getting entangled in negative exchanges with people in the first place. Over time you will sort the wheat from the chaff and become more able to decline new invitations to the negative dance.

Nobody is perfect and most relationships will have *some* negative mirroring in them. However, for the purposes of this book we are looking at the early stages of dating and if there are negative mirrors present then, it is a big red flag signalling low vibrations. A guy who is acting as a negative mirror will reveal himself very early on, if you know what to look out for and pay attention to what you notice. Most women who end up in painful relationships report that there were signs within the first two or three dates or even during the communications before they met a guy *but they chose to ignore or minimise it.*

When it comes to meeting new men and the early stages of dating, declining negative mirrors should be absolutely straightforward, though not necessarily any less challenging. This is because you have no 'real' emotional attachment to any man you have just started dating – and it is important that you keep it that way until you are *absolutely sure about him.* Be warned, it is easy to create a 'premature attachment' with a date and low self-esteem will give you a very strong desire to do so.

If you are currently single you are in a prime position for starting a new relationship on the right footing. This is to be both celebrated and taken full advantage of. Remember, we are not looking for Mr 'But I really Like Him' or Mr 'Will Do for Now'; we are looking for *Mr Wonderful.* There really is no hurry and it is important that you protect yourself by getting it right from the very beginning.

Learning to respond differently to mirrors will take some trial and error. It doesn't matter how far you are down the road of denial, you *can* learn to lovingly parent yourself: Start exactly where you are today and then take it one step at a time.

♥ How to Support Yourself in Changing Your Response to Mirrors:

1. Be patient and loving with yourself.
2. Always remember: *You are raising your vibration – not proving your worth.*
3. Avoid the 'chicken and egg' trap.
4. When having a wobble – connect to Source.
5. Change the focus of your efforts.
6. Accept that your search for love requires a change of consciousness.
7. Get the right support.

1. Be patient and loving with yourself

While it becomes much easier to say 'no thanks' once you are connected to Source and know you are intrinsically worthy, self love still takes practice – often a great deal of practice. The goal is not to become perfect or to berate your self for having low self-esteem as that would be completely counter productive. View this as a *process of reminding yourself* over and over while you gradually get better at declining negative mirrors. Sometimes you can do it straight away; sometimes you get caught out and have to go a little way along with a mirror before you can walk away. Sometimes you may get completely hooked and have to see a relationship all the way through to its painful, messy end. *This is all part of the learning process.*

It is really important that you aren't hard on yourself about making 'mistakes'. The first lesson in learning to lovingly parent ourselves is to acknowledge that our journey is about *progress not perfection*, and we learn to accept that we are all growing at different rates. Think of your self as a child learning a new skill rather than a machine who is there to do your bidding. *This is your soul's 'journey to love', not a quick fix.*

2. Always remember: *You are raising your vibration – not proving your worth*

You can decline a negative mirror without questioning your worth and without having to change a thing about it. This is what you must learn to do if you want to raise your vibration. *Your true worth cannot be proved or disproved; it can only be remembered or forgotten.* Negative mirrors only have the power to undermine our self-esteem and make us forget that we are lovable *if we choose to accept and internalise them.* And we only end up accepting them when we believe that they reflect our worth rather than our current vibration.

3. Avoid the chicken and egg trap

While you are learning to decline negative mirrors you can easily fall into the 'chicken and egg' trap if you secretly believe you can only *really* love yourself when others love you first: 'How can I love myself when no one loves me yet? How can I love myself when no one has shown me I am lovable? Who am *I* to say I am lovable? Doesn't someone else have to agree that I am ok first? What if I *really am* as awful as I suspect, or as people have made me feel I am? What if I *am* wrong and I do have to become 'better' before I can be lovable – won't people just keep showing me I am unlovable until I accept it and change? Can they really *all* be wrong about me?'

What we are really asking is: Can self love really come *before* we experience others truly loving us? Yes, it absolutely can. And everyone you have encountered so far *can* be wrong about you. *The only thing you have to change about yourself before you can receive love from others is your vibration – never the core of who you are.* If you have been practising connecting to Source Energy and raising your self-esteem/vibration, you may still have these self doubting questions pop up from time to time. That's ok, self doubt can be a stubborn habit to break. You are loveable, but not perfect.

♥ *Remember; everyone is lovable. Yes, everyone. You are not the special exception to the rule!*

We can choose to live in a negative vibration, *but that does not change our essential worth as human beings.* Those of us vibrating on a lower level have just forgotten who we really are and this can cause us to act a little (or very) dysfunctional at times. Other people are just the same as us, they forget too, and when they are operating from a low vibration they are unable to reflect your true worth back to you. If they have forgotten their own worth how can they possibly reflect love to you? Looking to a negative mirror to show us our worth really is expecting the blind to lead the blind.

♥ *Someone with low self-esteem cannot help anyone else raise their vibration because only someone with a high vibration is able to really mirror love.*

You can decide to bypass the chicken and egg mental loop altogether and create a brand new beginning; you can choose to become a person who is connected to Source and full to the brim with self-esteem, rather than one who waits for others to change before accepting that you are worthy of their love.

4. When having a wobble – connect to Source

While we are learning how to love ourselves, we will constantly need to remind ourselves to *consciously connect to Source*. It is all very well sitting in your bedroom connecting to Source when you are feeling good, or as part of your morning ritual but *the time you really need to do it is when you are having a wobble*. Use the easy times to practice creating the feeling and then start doing it when you are having a wobble. As with any new skills, this will take practice, and lots of it.

Mostly, when we have a wobble, we forget about everything except how awful we are feeling; we start to fall into the black hole. That is the crucial moment when your inner parent must throw down a ladder and guide you back to the solution – your connection to Source – so you can remember that you are worthy and loved. Sometimes we need to take time out to help us reconnect with our true self and with Source. We can go for a walk in nature, play with a pet or child, write in our journal, phone a friend or visit somewhere calm and inspiring like a church or temple. Sometimes it is enough to just stop any negative thoughts and evoke that yummy feeling on the spot. Whenever we experience a 'don't want' in our lives, we need to remind ourselves that we are worthy of what we *do* want.

♥ *Whenever we have lost sight of our Divine Self we must only remember to re-connect to Source.*

5. Change the focus of your efforts

A woman with wobbly self-esteem will often work extremely hard to bend and fit in with her man, so she can be liked and can therefore start to feel worthy of love. She will also work very hard at trying to make a relationship work, even when it's obvious to everyone around her that she is wasting her time and selling herself short. What would happen if we were to take the same incredible dedication and energy and spend it on practising saying 'no thanks' until it becomes second nature? If your strategy and effort hasn't worked up until now, then it might well be time to change tack. Even if you secretly think that nothing will make things any better – you at least owe it to yourself to *try* something different. After all, *what have you got to lose?*

6. Accept that your search for love requires a change of consciousness

Changing how you respond to a mirror is essentially very simple but can be incredibly challenging because it requires both a leap of faith and shift in consciousness. It requires a certain level of emotional maturity because you are stepping out of the child state of *passively accepting* what is mirrored around you and into the empowered adult state of *choosing* which mirrors you want to accept.

Children don't have the ability to be discerning because they are still developing and also because they *have* to blindly accept what is going on around them in order to survive. Those of us who experienced distorted (unloving) mirrors being held up to us by the adults we relied on as children often come to falsely believe life is being 'done to' us. We believe that the only way we can change the mirror is to become 'better' (more lovable or good) people and therefore we can become completely focused on pleasing others to gain approval. This, of course, only keeps us disempowered and locked in our low self-esteem. Remember; no matter how hard you try to be more acceptable to others, if inside you feel unlovable, that is the vibration you will be sending out into the Universe. And you can guarantee that belief will be confirmed over and over until *you* decide to change it.

7. Get the right support

Working through all of this on your own is not impossible, but it can make things more challenging. There are many ways to get support and

I would suggest it is well worth looking for people to share this journey with you. You can look for individual support through counselling or therapy, join a 12 Step group such as Co-Dependents Anonymous or start a MMW group so you can share this special journey with other women. Check the appendix for further information on support.

You may have friends or relatives with whom you can share this journey, but make sure that they are *really* supporting you and understand where you are coming from. You could try asking them to read this book and see what their reaction is.

When you are looking for support, the same rules apply as looking for Mr Wonderful – *notice how the 'support' makes you feel.* If you feel undermined *in any way* by your support, then it is not right for you and you need to look elsewhere. Trust your instincts on this.

Get started on raising your vibration right away – don't wait until someone will hold your hand while you do it. Once you have started you can investigate what other support you need along the way. *Ultimately your greatest support is Source.* All other support is brought to you by this Universal Energy. Ask Source for help. Ask Source to help you on your journey of self discovery. Practice re-connecting with Source on a daily basis; you will not only be gaining wonderful support, you will be raising your vibration.

So here are the key points about dealing with negative mirrors:

- If you are waiting for the negative mirrors to change before you change your view of yourself, you may be waiting forever. *You* will have to take responsibility for your beliefs and for changing them. If this is difficult at least 'act as if', get support and *get practising.*
- Do not be fooled into thinking negative mirrors reflect your worth as a human being. They only reflect your recent vibrational energy, which you are learning to raise. The negative mirrors will not disappear overnight, but they will lose their power over you as soon

as you accept they do not reflect your worth.

- Only positive mirrors should be accepted as reflecting your worth as a human being. They will of course multiply as soon as you start tuning into them. You have to know (or at least start acting as if) you are lovable to attract more loving vibrations from others.

- Keep the focus on learning how to love *yourself* rather than on working out how to 'love' men, (so that they would finally start to love you back; so that you can then feel ok...)

Essentially this process is about *changing how you feel*. To change how you feel, you first have to be willing to change what you *think*, what you *believe* about yourself and the world around you.

'Changing the way you feel' does *not* mean trying to fit in with things that go against your desires or your authentic self, nor does it mean trying to ignore or suppress negative feelings to make life easier. 'Changing how you feel' is simply about acknowledging you are a child of God: that you are *'of Source'* and, therefore, essentially worthy and lovable. You can *genuinely* feel good about yourself when you remember this and allow yourself the pleasure of experiencing your divine connection. Ultimately, nothing else really matters. Your life and relationships will improve beyond recognition once you are flowing *with* Source Energy.

You change the way you feel when you trust who you really are. This frees you to be able to *listen to what your feelings tell you and allow them to guide your choices in life*. When you feel bad about yourself (because you have forgotten who you are) you spend an inordinate amount of time and energy trying to feel better by looking *outside* of yourself. When you are dominated by your Big Black Hole in this way, *you are not free to tune into your feelings which are there to guide you*.

In terms of Manifesting Mr Wonderful, what you have been doing so far is creating a strong internal foundation. Without a strong core self we vibrate on a low level and what we attract into our lives will reflect this. *Changing the way you feel* will raise your vibration and the experiences you attract into your life. Once you have a handle on this you are ready to move on to trying out other self loving behaviours which is what we will explore next.

Putting Self Love into Action

If you are connecting to Source and changing the way you respond to mirrors you are ready to start practising other self loving behaviours. You can of course start practising these at any time, but if you are already creating a strong core you will find it easier. Having a connection to Source and a healthy relationship to vibrational mirrors comes first because they affect your core and without these two being sorted you will struggle in developing other self loving behaviours. Now you are ready, let's go back to the list:

♥ How to Love Your Self:

1. Know who you are (identity) and what is important to you (values)
2. Take your own needs and feelings into consideration when dealing with others
3. Believe you are deserving of the best treatment and respect from others
4. Know what your boundaries and limits are and know how to protect them
5. Enjoy your own company as well as spending time with others
6. Make sure that you do things that make you happy and bring you pleasure
7. Take good care of your physical needs for sleep, food, relaxation and exercise
8. Only get emotionally involved with people who treat you well
9. Allow yourself to make mistakes and be imperfect
10. Accept others as they are without having to change them (because you take responsibility for your own needs and stay out of harmful relationships)

1. Know who you are (identity) and what is important to you (values)

By now I hope you have some idea that you are a Divine Being. But who *else* are you? What makes you unique? We are all Divine Beings and we are all unique. Part of our journey is about figuring out who we are as individuals. Having a sense of identity is essential to being able to be in an equal, conscious relationship because you will need to have a self from which to relate to your partner.

Your values are equally important. Sometimes we aren't aware of our values and then we get a nagging feeling that something just doesn't 'fit' for us. *Our values are simply those things that are important to us.* They are sometimes related to our morals – but morals and values are not the same thing. Our moral values are the morals that are important to us. But we may also value 'spirituality' or 'city life' or 'healthy living'. They are not morals (judgments of right and wrong) but they can be equally important to us. It is crucial to be aware of what is important to us so we can ensure that our values are respected.

One of the fastest ways to become deeply unhappy is to go against your own values. If one of your values is 'honesty', then being with a man who doesn't mind stretching the truth to get his own way will probably make you feel uncomfortable. People with low self-esteem will readily put their values to one side to fit in with the other person. It is even possible to be unaware that you are doing this, which is why it is crucial that you identify your values, so that you can safeguard them.

♥ *Know thy self.*

If you read this and feel that you really don't have a clue who you are and/or what your values are, then it is time to find out! The following exercise can help you identify your values.

Activity 1

Answer the following questions in your journal and free write the answers. You can be both voices; the one asking the questions (coach) gets one colour pen and the one giving the answers (client) gets a different colour pen. Have a conversation with your self. Don't be afraid to ask those awkward questions or the ones that surface as you write your answers. Be creative and bold! Follow the questions where they want to go. If the idea of doing this on your own seems daunting you could begin the process with a life coach who can help you explore these questions in a structured way. (Counselling can also help, but isn't always so structured.) You could also ask a friend to take it in turns with you asking the questions and sharing the answers.

Ask yourself the following questions;
- Who am I?
- What is important to me?
- What couldn't I live without?
- What are my strengths?
- What kind of lifestyle suits me best?
- What do I want to be remembered for when I die?
- If I only had three years to live what would I do?
- Who or what 'grates' against me in my life right now?

These are very open-ended questions designed to make you think deeply. If you are using the questions for journaling, let the answers flow freely – don't censor. Don't worry about spelling – just respond. Keep writing until you can't think of anything else to write. Then, with the other colour pen, write *another* question that comes up from the answer given. Be probing. Imagine you are a psychologist doing detective work.

Here is an example of using the questions in journaling:

(Coach Self) What couldn't you live without?
(Client self) Oh, chocolate! I couldn't live without a supply of quality chocolate. I also couldn't live without my astrology books and crystals because I use them all the time. I also need some peace and quiet in the evening. I like to be able to wind down when I get home from work.

How long do you need to unwind?
Well, on a stressful day – sometime a whole evening. But most of the time I only need an hour or so.

What do you like to do when you are unwinding in peace and quiet?
Sometimes I just like to sit there and think or write my journal. Other times I like to read, or have a relaxing bath. I am rather into watching rom com DVDs at the moment too. I'd like to be able to say yoga or meditation… but the truth is I am more likely to go for an evening walk than get the yoga mat out!

So what is the most important aspect of this peace and quiet?
That no one is asking anything of me or demanding my attention. I don't mind sharing time with someone else around – as long as I can relax. I do, however need some time to myself with my own thoughts. Having someone else there is ok – as long as I can be silent.

So would you say silence is more important than being on your own?
I do need some alone time, but as long as I can go inside myself and not have to think about another person – whether I am silent or watching a film doesn't matter. So I would say not having to always verbally communicate is important to me.

Through this (genuine) journaling dialogue I have managed to identify 'not having to verbally communicate all the time' as one of my values. You can use any of the above questions to find out more about your own identity and values. Once you have identified a value, add it to a list. Values do change over time and in different circumstances, but it is really essential to recognise them *and* to pay attention when you are being asked by someone to ignore your values.

2. Take your own needs and feelings into consideration when dealing with others

Women with high self-esteem know that they are worthy of consideration. You are just as important as anyone else. However, in your own life, *you* are the most important person to take care of. If you are not functioning well because you are ignoring your needs and feelings, then you will also be of little use to anyone else and have little to give others. Have you ever been on an plane when they give the safety instructions? The passengers are instructed to see to their own masks before helping anyone else – even a child. If we sort ourselves out first, we are in a stronger position to be there for others. It is not selfish to take care of yourself – on the contrary – *you are the only person in the world who has this responsibility*. No one else can (or should) do it for you, so you *must* do it for yourself.

If you have low self-esteem you may believe that you are worth less consideration than others. (Hopefully by now you are beginning to see that this is just not true.) You may habitually worry about others' feelings and needs and ignore your own, often without even knowing you're doing it. Worse still, low self-esteem can make us tell ourselves that we don't *deserve* to be considered. We may end up feeling chronically guilty or ashamed when we do decide to think about ourselves. Denigrating yourself does not make you more 'worthy' in the eyes of others and it certainly does not encourage others to look after your needs – except sometimes out of guilt. You are not being 'caring' or 'selfless' by denigrating your wonderful self; you are secretly hoping to make people like and approve of you so you can start to feel better about yourself.

♥ *No one wants you to be a doormat unless they were hoping to wipe their feet on you.*

If you have a long history of ignoring your needs and feelings, it is time to take responsibility for your Self and do something about it. There are other, healthier ways to feel better about your self than trying to ignore your needs and feelings in favour of others. If you have surrounded yourself with 'feet wipers' (people who enjoy taking advantage of you), then this may take some time and effort to change because *they won't want you to.* Be prepared for the fact that there will always be people who will try to make you feel guilty and ashamed about taking care of your self instead of them. When someone behaves like this they are acting as a negative mirror *which you can choose to decline.* You need to be strong and know that you deserve the same level of consideration as anyone else.

If you have started the process of building your self-esteem, then changing the way you relate to your needs and feelings will gradually become easier. But remember, it takes time to break habits – be gentle and loving with yourself while you go through this process of transforming from a willing doormat into a worthy Divine Being.

3. Believe you deserve the best treatment and respect from others

Once you begin to consider your own needs and feelings, you will naturally start to expect others to *also* consider you and to treat you with respect. Once you become better at taking care of your own needs and listening to how you feel, it will naturally follow that others will become more willing to respect you. *When you respect someone, you pay attention to them and you hold them in high esteem.* It is much harder to respect someone who is denigrating themselves. If someone demonstrates self-respect, it attracts others who are respectful because you are vibrating on a higher level.

It is worth noting that when a person respects your needs and feelings they are not putting you above themselves, they are just *considering* you. It is important that we don't confuse *the consideration of* needs/feelings with *responsibility for* needs/feelings. Each and every (functioning) adult is responsible for their own needs/feelings but we can also pay attention to other people's needs/feelings during our dealings with them. When someone respects us it doesn't always mean that we will not ever be hurt or disappointed by them – it just means that we have been considered in the situation.

As a woman who has high self-esteem, you have a healthy self respect and are only interested in being around people who treat you well. You are looking for positive mirrors and declining negative ones. Disrespect of any sort is a negative mirror. Remember, if someone disrespects you, it has nothing to do with your intrinsic worth. However, if you decide to *accept* the disrespectful behaviour, it is a sign that you *believe you are unworthy*.

It is not uncommon for women with low self-esteem to not even *recognise* disrespectful behaviour in themselves or others. It is something that you may have to learn by trial and error. If you were badly treated as a child, there may be a lot of confusion about what constitutes 'bad treatment' because disrespect may have been normal in your family. It is never too late to learn what respect is.

We will be looking at the kind of behaviour that is unacceptable from a date in the next chapter but for the time being, be aware that if someone makes you feel guilty, ashamed, punished, judged, angry or anxious, there is a good chance that they are doing you a disservice. Your job is to listen to and pay attention to your feelings – they will guide you in your relationships.

Sometimes we can feel 'bad' around someone because their energy does not gel with ours and it makes us feel uncomfortable. If we experience bad feelings around someone, then it is not a good idea to spend a lot of time with them, regardless of whether or not they are being disrespectful. Our feelings may simply be telling us the other person is not a good energy match for us.

4. Know what your boundaries and limits are and how to protect them

As you get to know yourself better you will become increasingly aware of what you are comfortable with and what you are not. A boundary is an invisible line that separates you from others. When it is crossed you feel uncomfortable. We have physical, emotional and sexual boundaries and we must learn to recognise where ours lie and find ways to protect them from being inadvertently or deliberately violated by others.

♥ *Our boundaries define what we are willing to experience and our limits define what we are willing to give.*

Physical Boundaries define our physical body and personal space. It has to do with how close someone can stand or sit next to us and how/when we like to be touched by others. When someone stands too close we feel uncomfortable because they are crossing an invisible physical boundary. This boundary is flexible according to the circumstances and people involved. You may feel comfortable with one friend holding your hand or hugging you – but not another. Remember it is *your* boundary, so *you* decide what feels comfortable. No one else can decide where your personal boundaries should lie.

Emotional boundaries and limits define how we like to conduct our relationships. We may be happy to listen to a friend cry and give her emotional support when she has just had a difficult loss. We may *not* feel comfortable with the same friend moving into our house for three months because of a break up, or ringing us every night about her problems. We may be happy to listen to our date talk about his last relationship in broad terms, but we may not want to know about how he used to feel about her or what they used to do together. We may be happy to give a friend an expensive birthday present but not feel comfortable lending them £100.

Sexual boundaries are not the same as physical boundaries because *they are not always physical in nature.* A look, a comment or a gesture can be sexually invasive. Sexual boundaries are highly *energetic* – and sexual energy is incredibly powerful. This is why when someone fancies us, we can often feel the intensity of their energy *even if they never touch us or speak to us.* It is also why it is incredibly uncomfortable when a sexual boundary is crossed, whether or not anything *physical* occurs.

Sexual violations are energetic and go straight to your Core. If you are getting an 'icky' feeling or sexual energy off someone that is unwanted then they are invading your sexual boundaries just as much as if they put their hand on your breast or up your skirt. If you have ever been leered at by a man you will know exactly what I am talking about. He doesn't have to do or say anything to make you feel he is being inappropriately sexual towards you. If a sexual boundary is crossed it often causes us to feel shame or disgust. Either we find the person disgusting or 'creepy' or sometimes they cause *us* to feel dirty.

You know a boundary is being invaded or crossed because it will make *you feel uncomfortable*. The uncomfortable feeling response can range from mild irritation to intense rage. It is also common to feel shame (that there is something wrong with or bad about you) when someone *deliberately* crashes your boundaries or tries to hurt you. *This is because we take this mirror to be reflecting something about us and our worth.* We take it *personally*. If someone does this they are acting as a negative mirror. We must remember that we are a worthy being, and disengage from them.

Obviously not everyone who crosses your boundaries is doing it deliberately or even consciously. What is essential is that *you* recognise when a boundary is being violated, regardless of whether or not they are doing it deliberately. Once you have acknowledged that someone is crossing your personal line, it is your responsibility to make your boundary clear. One of the most effective ways to protect your boundaries is to practice saying 'no thanks'. Being able to say to someone 'that makes me feel uncomfortable' or 'I don't feel comfortable with that' or 'please stop doing that' or simply 'stop' is crucial. Sometimes you simply need to walk away from a person or situation.

Saying 'no thanks' can be extremely challenging, especially for women. We can suffer guilt, shame, and fear when we choose how we want to relate to others. Sometimes we may experience abusive reactions when we practice standing up for ourselves or we may take it too far and become defensively aggressive to give us more of a sense of power. This is all part of the process and we must persevere through the challenge. When setting boundaries; start with the small things that don't matter so much. Keep practising until you no longer go into a tail spin when you think your boundaries have been crashed.

♥ *It is up to you to protect and care for your own self by respecting your boundaries and limits.*

5. Enjoy both your own company and spending time with others

Enjoying your own company *and* the company of others are a really good sign that you are filling up with Source Energy and that your self-esteem is brimming over. When we don't like ourselves we often don't like our own company because it makes us feel empty and lonely. Sometimes with low self-esteem we *prefer* isolating ourselves because being around others reminds us of how awful we secretly feel. Whether we are avoiding being alone or being with others, what we are really doing is trying to avoid the black hole.

As you develop a healthy self-esteem by connecting to the Source, the black hole shrinks and you start to feel less internal pain. This enables you to spend time nurturing your relationships both with yourself and with others.

Activity 2

1. Try exploring these questions through journaling or with a therapist/coach; I recommend that you do this even if you think you are already doing ok – it may stretch you further!

- Which one do you struggle with most? (Solitude or company)
- Has it always been like this for you?
- If not, how has it changed over the years?
- List all the things you prefer doing on your own:
- List all the things you prefer doing with other people:

- List all the things you are happy doing alone or with others:
- Are there any things you have never done alone?
- Are there any things you have never shared/done with others?

2. Now, *choose one thing you have never done by yourself or one thing you have never done with others and try it! (It's ok to go for the least scary activity.)*

3. When you have done it, answer the following questions:

- How did it go?
- Would you do it again?
- Is there anything else you could try from your list?
- What else can you do develop yourself in the area you feel most challenged? (Solitude or company)

6. Make sure that you do things that make you happy and bring you pleasure

(I *love* this one!) When we feel down on ourselves this idea can seem pointless, unimportant or indulgent. Do not be fooled.

♥ *Happiness and pleasure are what we are here to experience.*

There is simply *nothing* more important than enjoying your life and doing things that make you feel good. If everyone made a point of doing this regularly we would live in a much more relaxed world. Instead, we slog away like work mules doing jobs we hate 'for the money' and then zone out from our misery in front of the TV on weeknights and with copious amounts of alcohol or shopping at the weekend. This is not living; it is surviving – *with props*.

Pleasure is the one great benefit of having a physical body on this amazing planet. It's what angels are envious of! Yes, we have to deal with the harsh realities of death and disappointment, but we certainly do *not* have to deny ourselves pleasure. In fact, pleasure will raise your vibration like nothing else. It connects you to the Source and to your authentic self because *when you are experiencing pleasure you are open and receptive.*

What is pleasure? Anything that makes you *smile.* It may be indulging in your senses – watching a beautiful sunset, listening to a favourite album, savouring a delicious sticky pudding, enjoying a sensual massage or bath, or smelling the roses in a park. It may be about sharing with others – having a laugh with some friends, playing with children, petting an animal, listening to an older relative tell a story. It may be about enjoying a solitary activity like painting, reading a good book or going for a walk; the list is endless. Try writing your own list: What do you love doing? What gives you pleasure? Keep adding to the list and make sure you enjoy something pleasurable *every single day.*

Pleasure is all about *being present in the moment.* Aside from doing things that you love, you can increase your pleasure in life by changing the way you think. You can decide to have pleasure while you are cleaning the bath. Once it is done, you can stand and smile while you admire your work and your lovely clean bath. There are things that are a chore – things that we dislike doing but know we have to do – but this should be only a small part of what we do with our lives. Is there anything you are doing that you needn't bother with?

We can also find ways to make the things we have to do more pleasurable for ourselves. Sometimes we need a reward for getting on with something we find difficult or demanding – and by that I don't mean using a prop to anesthetise ourselves from a life lacking in pleasure. Work should be a pleasure and it really *can* be. Sometimes a change of attitude is all that's required.

Sometimes a change of job is necessary – sticking with a permanent, full time job you hate *just* for the money really is fate worse than death. You are here on this planet *today* and all of our days here on this planet are numbered. Whatever you do, don't resign yourself to wasting years of your precious life on a job you hate or on doing tasks you can get away with not doing.

7. Take good care of your physical needs for sleep, food, relaxation and exercise

Although this one sounds pretty simple and obvious, a surprising number of people fail to take care of at least one of these basic needs. Often when we are stressed these will be the first to suffer. Meeting these basic needs will form part of the foundation you are building for your core self. You could be doing all the self-esteem building exercises in the world, but if you ignore or skimp on your body's physical needs you will undermine your good work. Taking care of yourself includes looking after your wonderful body and her health. If you are lacking in more than one of these areas tackle one at a time.

Sleep

A lack of sleep will make you stressed, more likely to get ill, and less able to cope with what life throws at you. Many people have problems sleeping when they are stressed, which of course usually only *adds* to the stress and creates a vicious cycle. However, more often than not, people just don't get to bed on time.

Everyone needs different amounts of sleep. I need around 9 hours to feel fully replenished which can be awkward when I have to get up early. When I was a school teacher I had to go to bed at 9.30 to get enough sleep and so I had to adjust my social life. I would make the odd exception but I would usually manage to get to bed on time because I knew I couldn't function with a lack of sleep and teaching was a particularly demanding job. If you don't already know how much sleep you need, take the time to find out.

Once you know how much sleep you need, give yourself a bed time and try to stick to it – allowing for the odd occasion when you *choose* to be up later. If you can't ever seem to get to bed on time, try to spend some quality time winding down in bed or in your bedroom thirty minutes before you plan to go to sleep. You can also try having a nap when you get home from work so that you can stay up a bit later. The trick is to find what works for you and create a healthy sleep routine that you can follow.

If you are having problems getting to or staying asleep then you need to acknowledge that you are either stressed or doing things that are hindering your sleep. Which is it? Are you drinking too much coffee/alcohol, eating too late or are you worrying about something? Sometimes we just need more time to wind down and get in the mood for sleep. I have discovered that if I write directly before I go to bed I have ideas going around in my head and I can't switch off. I now make sure that even if I write in the evening, that I spend an hour or two doing something else before I go to bed like having a bath, reading a book or watching a film. Sometimes all you need is to take your mind down a gear or two before trying to sleep.

It is worth investigating what is causing any sleep problems and doing whatever you can to solve it – even if it means you have to try out several things before you come up with a solution. If you are stressed then you will need to find ways to calm your mind and relax. Yoga, meditation, walking, exercise and dealing with emotional problems in counselling are all proven ways to de-stress. Check your diet and your bedtime routine to see if you are inadvertently doing something that is keeping you awake. You may even be overtired. Sometimes getting to sleep is hardest when you really need to and you know that you have to get up early. If you are chilling out before trying to sleep and going to bed within your bedtime, this is less likely to happen.

Food
Food and our relationship to it is a huge topic so let's keep it simple:

- Eat if you are hungry.
- Make sure you get enough of what you need in terms of vitamins, minerals and different food types.
- Try to avoid eating/drinking what you know doesn't agree with *your* body. (Listen to your body; she will tell you when she doesn't feel comfortable with something, even if you like the taste.)
- Have a little of what you like, even if you think it is 'fattening'. Being overly strict with yourself about food only makes you more

likely to binge later because you feel deprived.

- Avoid using food (or alcohol) to 'reward' yourself. By all means *allow yourself something nice to eat or drink*, but if you use food/alcohol to reward yourself for something then you are encouraging a dysfunctional relationship with food/alcohol. (If you associate something as being a 'reward' you will naturally want more of it because it makes you feel 'good'.) Many of us already have this association because when we were children, adults used food to reward or punish us. *Food is a basic need that should also be enjoyed.* It should *never* be used to control behaviour in yourself or others.

- The key to eating is 'moderation in everything' unless your body doesn't feel comfortable with it – in which case you should find an alternative.

- If you think you have any serious issues with food seek professional help or join a food related 12 Step programme.

Relaxation

Relaxation is more than sleeping or resting. It is giving our self a chance to simply *be*. When we are busy and productive we often forget that we actually inhabit a body and that we have a wonderful opportunity to experience just being here on this amazing planet. There is nothing wrong with forgetting or being busy just as long as we take time to come back to ourselves and we need to be relaxed to do this. We can relax alone or we can share our being-ness with others. Whichever way we chose to relax, it is important that we do so regularly and that we put our worries and chores to one side while we do it.

Exercise

Exercise is not just about keeping the pounds off. Exercise is essential to the smooth running of our bodies, particularly as we get older. It also has the added benefit of helping us to de-stress and relax. It gives us a sense of well being and can help us develop a healthy enjoyment of our body. As with many things, moderation is the key. If you want to get super fit, make sure you build up to it slowly and don't over do it.

One of the most fantastic ways to exercise is to walk. You can stretch your arms and legs, blow out the cobwebs, push it up a gear or two to get your pulse going *and* enjoy the view as you do it. Walking can be gentle or get you to break into a sweat if you go fast enough. It is also weight bearing, which means it is good for your bones. You don't have to pay for it and you don't need any fancy equipment. All you have to do is go out and put one foot in front of the other while heading in a pleasant direction... How easy is that?

Another good way to exercise is to incorporate physical activity into your normal day. If you commute to work, why not walk or cycle at least some of the way? If you drive a car, why not park half a mile from work and walk the last part? If you work or live off the ground floor, run (or walk) up the stairs. If you have an hour for lunch, why not spend half of it taking a stroll in a park or around the block? Use the car as little as possible. Walk or cycle for all your local trips and you will not only benefit your health but you will save money *and* benefit the environment too. It also means you won't have to take so much time to go to the gym or pool – unless of course you enjoy going.

Exercise, like most things, should be fun and pleasurable. Find a way to incorporate it into you life that feels *good*. Play tennis or badminton with friends or go for a bike ride if the treadmill fills you with dread and loathing. If you can, add a spa into the equation if you have to go to the gym or pool. Make it part of your quality time with yourself.

♥ *Your body loves to be active and to be taken care of.*

8. Only get emotionally involved with people who treat you well

We can't always determine who is in our life. We may have work colleagues, neighbours, family and even people in our social circle who we would rather weren't there. Unfortunately, they often have just as much right to be there as you. We can't always avoid or 'cut out' challenging people from our lives. We can, however, determine *how deeply involved* we get with them.

♥ *We are really in trouble when we allow someone to be close to us when they treat us badly.*

When we realise we have a choice – that we can freely choose who we get emotionally involved with – it can be quite a revelation. When we were children we had little choice about whom we relied on and with whom we spent most of our time. One of the great benefits of being a grown-up is that we get to choose the level of involvement in our relationships.

This is where responsibility for ourselves comes in – it is important that we make an assessment of people we want to get emotionally involved with to decide if they treat us properly. If they don't, we can simply choose to keep our distance. We can avoid spending a lot of time with them. We can decide not to get into a sexual relationship with them. We can decide to divorce them. We can choose not to confide in them or ask anything of them.

We *always* have a choice about whether we remain emotionally involved – even if the person is family. Family have no more right to treat you badly than anyone else! It is definitely more complex to sort out family relationships but you can start by strengthening your boundaries and making your limits clear. You don't always have to cut people off – you just have to be willing to stand up for and to protect yourself. Sometimes, however, you may have to cut someone out of your life if they insist on treating you badly and they don't respect your boundaries or limits.

You know some one is treating you well if:
- You know that they like you.
- You know that they care about your needs and feelings.
- You know that they respect your boundaries.
- You know they are on your side and supportive.

- They make an effort for you.
- They show up for you.
- They make you feel good about yourself and about being with them.

If someone makes you feel bad, don't get emotionally involved with them. Protect yourself from negative mirrors and look for people who make you feel like the worthy person you are.

9. Allow yourself to make mistakes and be imperfect

A perfect human is an oxymoron. We are by our very nature imperfect. However, when we feel bad about ourselves we often falsely believe that if we reach for perfection we will find a way to feel better about ourselves. When we reach for perfection we are seeking conditional love – love based on approval. As we have already discussed, low self-esteem has to do with *forgetting who we truly are*. When we aim for perfection we only take ourselves *further away* from our authentic selves.

We are perfectly imperfect. We are Divine Beings that reside in limited physical bodies and with a complex, flawed personality which has both strengths and weaknesses. We are 'sinners' not because we are intrinsically bad but because we are naturally *imperfect*. We make mistakes because we are *supposed* to make mistakes, not because there is something wrong with us. By all means strive to be your best Self and aim to learn from your mistakes. However, avoid measuring yourself against the illusion of perfection because you will always fall short and have something to feel bad about. Give your self the unconditional love you deserve.

10. Accept others as they are without having to change them (because you take responsibility for your own needs and stay out of harmful relationships)

Changing other people is impossible. People *always* change themselves. Someone may love you deeply but their feeling for you won't make them change if they are not ready to. It is nothing personal. And it certainly isn't a reflection of your worth.

Trying to change another person is a waste of energy. It simply doesn't work. All it will do is prolong your misery and annoy them. If you are focused on someone else, then you are not focused on yourself. If you are not focused on yourself you will become more and more estranged from Source Energy and will feel depressed, angry and/or powerless. You *are* powerless over others so trying to change them is the same as banging your head on a brick wall.

♥ *You are never powerless over your relationship with yourself.*

All you can do is make sure you remain steadfastly true to yourself. You won't feel the need to change others if you are taking care of your own needs, because you won't be expecting others to do it for you. And you won't feel the need to change others if you only get involved with trustworthy people who make you feel good about being *you*.

If you find yourself involved with someone you really want to change, bring the focus back to yourself. Take better care of your own needs. Build your self-esteem by connecting with Source. Protect your boundaries and respect your own limits. Use the 'no' word. Go and talk things over with a counsellor. When you change the focus of your energy back to your relationship with yourself you will discover whether or not you can work things out with the other person.

♥ *Once you are taking good care of yourself, it becomes easier to accept others the way they are.*

Sometimes we have to leave people behind and it may be sad or painful. You can accept them for who they are and decide not to get or remain involved with them. Accepting others is not the same as agreeing to be involved with them when you know they won't make you happy. That is refusing to acknowledge the truth and secretly hoping one day they will change. That won't make either of you happy in the long run.

Activity 3

1. Take the previous list of 10 loving actions. Check each loving action and give yourself a score between 0-10 on how well you think you are doing in the present. 0 means you don't ever do it, 10 means there really is no room for improvement; you are already doing great!

2. Next, list the loving actions you are strongest in and the ones you need to improve the most. Anything that scores under 7 or 8 will be actively undermining your efforts to develop your self-esteem. (The lower the score the greater the impact.)

3. Choose one loving action from your 'needs to improve' list to work on first. It doesn't have to be the one you have the most difficulty with, but do choose a lower scoring item.

4. For a minimum of one week, journal how you do with this on a daily basis. Give yourself a score each day and write down what went well and what didn't go so well. All you are doing is *observing* yourself. This is not about judging yourself; it's about raising your awareness so you can become more able to change the way you do things. (Remember – change takes time.)

5. You can repeat this process for another week or, if you feel you have enough information, read about it again and decide if there is anything that has been suggested that you would like to try. If not, then list your own suggestions. This is only a brief overview of each loving action. If you feel you need more information, then go out there and find it! (Check appendix for further resources.)

6. Write down what you are going to do *and when you are going to do it* – put it in your diary. Give yourself clear goal/s so you can measure your improvements.

7. When you feel ready you can move onto another loving action on your 'needs to improve' list and repeat the process.

8. Review the list at 6 monthly intervals and again give yourself scores for each loving action.

9. Decide if you need to repeat the weekly journal exercise with any of the loving actions to help you break a challenging behaviour

pattern.

10. Make sure you reward yourself for any improvements or goals met. (Don't use food or alcohol – buy yourself something frivolous or go for a nice massage instead.)

Chapter 4

Designing

Transforming the Way You Date

What Kind of Relationship Do You Really Want?

When you begin dating, it is important to have a good idea about what you want. In order to get a clear picture, you also need to be sure about what you *don't* want. In this chapter we will explore various aspects of the 'dating dance' between men and women. You will discover what you need to do to raise your energy vibration and maximise your chances of attracting the right man for you.

While your feelings are always going to be your ultimate guide in relationships, it can be helpful to have some guidance. Imagine you are going mushroom-picking. Of course you will need your *senses* (poisonous mushrooms often smell bad) but you *also* need to know what signs to look out for. Eating the wrong kind of mushroom can be fatal. Letting the wrong guy into your life can be emotionally catastrophic, so you owe it to yourself to make sure you're well-informed before you take a bite!

In terms of raising your vibration, it is better to have no attention at all than to accept the wrong sort. The minute you realise that a man is giving you the wrong sort of attention *it is time to let him go, even if there is no one else on the horizon.* Keeping your options open is a good dating strategy, especially if you are prone to 'falling' too fast, but that doesn't mean being open to *any* option, even as a distraction. Some male attention is just plain bad news, even if it seems on the surface to be bolstering your self-esteem or simply a 'bit of fun'.

The most common barrier to manifesting Mr Wonderful is wasting your energy on men who won't give you what you want. If he isn't giving you the right sort of attention then he is essentially unavailable, *even if you are the only woman he is dating.* The time to let your guard down is when you are sure you are receiving the right attention, so it is important that you can recognise Mr Unavailable in all his guises.

Common Varieties of Mr Unavailable

- Mr Sexual
- Mr Non-Committal
- Mr Mixed Messages
- Mr Controlled
- Mr Passionate
- Mr Power Games

Δ Mr Sexual

We all want to be seen as attractive and sexy. As heterosexual women, sexual attention from a man can be very seductive, especially if he knows what he is doing. However, if a man lets us know he thinks we are sexually attractive, it isn't always as much of a compliment as you might think. A man finding you attractive (or sexy) on its own actually means *very little.* Of course, Mr Wonderful will find you attractive – but not every man who finds you attractive will have something to offer you.

According to John Gray in *Mars and Venus on a Date,*[1] men are generally not overly discerning about which women they find attractive. A man may really fancy and even want to see sleep with you but that doesn't automatically mean he wants to have a relationship with you. And even if he *does* want to get involved, it doesn't mean that he is emotionally available or that what he has to offer will be what you want. Men usually find *many* women sexy, it's in their nature. Mr Wonderful will know to be respectful about how and when he shows his attraction to you – Mr Sexual, on the other hand, *won't.*

Women can easily mistake male sexual attention for the offer of love. It is an extremely common misunderstanding which is partly due to the differences between men and women. In *Mars and Venus on a Date* (see appendix), John Gray explains that men are like blow torches; they heat up quickly and can switch off just as suddenly, often baffling the object of their once heated desire. Women, who take longer to warm up, are naturally more discerning about whom they become sexually attracted to and so can easily mistake sexual attraction from a man for more than it actually is. This difference poses particular problems for women who suffer low self-esteem because the desire to be loved can interfere in her ability to be discerning. And of course, Mr Sexual targets women who take sexual attention as a huge compliment because they don't have a very high opinion of themselves.

For women who have been sexually abused this can be further complicated by confused messages about love and sex. If a woman was sexually abused by a man (as a child) then it can become very difficult to say no to overtly sexual advances as an adult, especially if the person who abused her was in a position of trust. Though it is true some women who have been abused may avoid sexual relationships, many have the opposite problem. When Mr Sexual comes along and shows he is attracted, she may respond automatically and find it very difficult to say no. She may even be triggered into responding with strong sexual desire herself. It wouldn't matter if he was completely inappropriate or unavailable – the sexual attention can seem to her to be the 'promise of love' which she may have great difficulty in refusing.

In order to manifest Mr Wonderful you need to accept that although many men may find you attractive, not every one of them is a potential partner. It is crucial to realise that if what a man is initially offering is *overtly sexual* then *you shouldn't even give him one chance*. He isn't actually offering you anything but sex and that is highly unlikely to change. Don't fall into the trap of accepting purely sexual attention – regardless of whether you intend to actually get physical with him or not. If the energy a man is sending you is sexual, he is coming from a fundamentally low (base) vibration. (This is of course the same for women.) There is nothing wrong with this if it is what you ultimately want. However, engaging in indiscriminate sexual behaviour will not lead you to Mr Wonderful.

You may believe you are being complimented when a man flirts or offers you sex. You may also think that this is his way of saying that he wants a relationship with you. However, just because he finds you attractive and would have sex with you it doesn't mean that he wants to get emotionally involved with you or give you his commitment.

You may also believe that once he has had sex with you that you may well be able to woo him with the promise of more. You may offer the best sex in the world but few men would ultimately choose a life partner based on sex alone. And if he did – would you really want *him*? Just because men love having sex with women it doesn't mean that they will give their heart to the 'sexiest' woman they meet.

Mr Wonderful makes you feel good; he is respectful and concerned with your happiness and comfort. In short, he is thinking about *you* rather than his sexual appetite. A man can show his appreciation for you by paying you a (non sexual) compliment or by asking you out. He really is not giving you much of a compliment by letting you know how much he would like to get you into bed because men who are that forward are rarely fussy – they take what they can get.

Mr Sexual might like to think he is paying you a massive compliment that you should gratefully receive, but what he is really doing is hedging his bets. He wants to get you into bed or enjoy flirting with you because it fulfils *his* needs or desires; you don't actually come into the picture, except in his sexual fantasies. And being a man's sexual fantasy is really not much of a compliment – except of course if you are planning a career as a porn star.

Many of you will be wondering if there's anything wrong with some 'harmless' flirting or casual sex. You need to ask yourself if it is really as harmless as you would like to believe. Some flirting is about enjoying being alive and celebrating the company you are in. It can be a social lubricant, even between people of the same sex. Flirting doesn't *have* to be sexual. If a man is flirting with you ask yourself the following:

• Is he available for a relationship? (If not, then why is he flirting with you and why are you accepting it?)

- Is he being respectful and friendly in the way he flirts or is he being overtly sexual?
- Is he giving you mixed messages or do you know exactly where you stand with him?

Any overtly sexual flirting, *especially* when he is unavailable, not interested in taking you out, or giving you mixed signals is a sign that he is operating on a purely sexual level and that he has dodgy sexual boundaries. Both of these mean that he is Mr Sexual and you need to avoid getting into an energetic exchange with him because *it will lower your vibration*. However, if he is an available man who is being playful rather than sexual *and* he is giving a consistent message then it is unlikely to be harmful – unless of course he doesn't get around to asking you out!

If you want sex rather than a loving relationship, then by all means enjoy the advances of Mr Sexual. I am making no moral judgement about overt sexual flirting or casual sex, if that is what you really want. However, do not make the mistake of believing that sexual energy (overt flirting or casual sex) will lead you to or help you 'catch' Mr Wonderful. Going along with a man's overt sexual attention may lead you into a relationship of sorts, but it is highly unlikely to be with Mr Wonderful.

What if *you* really want sex? Perhaps you are rationalising that you don't want a *relationship* with Mr Sexual and are happy to just have a one night stand or a fling with him? When you choose a purely sexual exchange, then *you are playing the role of Ms Sexual*. It is impossible to seriously work on raising your vibration when you are engaging in casual sex. You are giving the Universe the very clear message that all you really want is sex, so that is what you are likely to attract. If you want to manifest a loving relationship, you need to make sure your energetic vibration is heart-centred.

Δ Mr Non Committal

Some men want to have the attention of women, or perhaps one particular woman, but they have absolutely nothing to offer or are terrified of having a real relationship. These men can often be found instant messaging, texting, emailing and browsing the internet like there is no tomorrow. However, he will not get around to asking you out, keep changing his mind at the last minute or never let it go very far. Ultimately he likes to browse because it is low risk and he gets to feel his life is full of female interest. Mr Non Committal is happy living in a fantasy world because it is safe. He never has to make any effort or to put himself on the line and risk rejection.

Mr Wonderful knows that if he wants the chance to get to know you then he has to ask you out and pay you proper attention. So, if a man sends you a non-descript first message like 'how R U?', 'Wot U up 2?', 'like your pic', or 'hey girls – any one fancy a chat?' then don't waste your precious energy replying. This is really not the sort of male attention you want to be attracting or accepting. Remember – what you accept is what you attract more of. If he can't be bothered to strike up a proper conversation with you, ignore him. If he doesn't ask you out within four (decent) email messages, stop replying; he is living in a fantasy world and/or wasting your time.

Δ Mr Mixed Messages

Some men will flirt or even ask you out and give you the impression they like you one minute, then they will do or say something that leaves you wondering 'was I imagining something going on?' or 'what is really happening here?' This guy is similar to Mr Non Committal, the difference is that you actually get to spend time and become involved with this guy. Lucky you! While you may become emotionally or sexually involved with Mr Mixed Messages, you can never feel secure about him or work out what is really going on. Here are some examples of Mr Mixed Message's antics:

- He may ask you out but then act like you are friends rather than on a date.
- He may ask you out and then turn out to have a girlfriend or wife.

- He may invite you out, but always with a group of friends or when it is convenient because he is just slotting you into what he was going to be doing anyway.
- He may ignore you one minute and flirt with you the next, depending on his mood.
- He may come on sexually strong one minute and then back off the next.
- He may be quite happy to get sexually involved with you but then not seem to have any time to spend with you doing other things.
- He may give you the impression that he has ended a relationship or intends to but then talks about the other woman all the time or changes his mind about what's actually going on.
- On the website *Facebook* he would probably describe his relationship situation as being 'complicated' or he would like to think of *himself* as being 'complicated'. (Yawn!)
- He may be on the rebound and honest about it, even soliciting your support for his wounded feelings.
- He may talk openly about feeling ambivalent about getting involved in a relationship or worse still, about his feelings for you.
- He may be 'open' about his confused feelings and seek sympathy or attention for them (which you are supposed to be flattered by) or he could be uncommunicative and leave you completely in the dark. Either way you never really know where you stand with him but he gives you just enough to make you think it may be worth hanging in there for the ultimate prize – his love!

It can be really painful trying to be in any sort of relationship with Mr Mixed Messages because he either blows hot and cold or behaves in a confusing way. He may like to give you the impression that he is 'scared' or confused but he is *more than happy to accept your attention*. Mr Mixed Messages actually gets off on your patient and/or desperate attention because it makes him feel powerful and wanted. He is more than happy to spend time with you when it suits him, and have you hankering for his attention when it doesn't.

Mr Mixed Messages is basically using you. He is offering you absolutely nothing except the 'opportunity' to pander to his needs while he either 'makes up his mind' or 'gets over' some emotional episode. If you agree to this kind of warped attention from Mr Mixed Messages you are agreeing to focus on meeting his needs on the off chance that you will gain his love/trust/attention/commitment at some point in the future. He will have no compunction about keeping you waiting even if he tells you openly that he is worried that he 'might hurt you'. Saying this just lets him off the hook when he does.

Mr Wonderful is available and ready to love you *today*. Mr Mixed Messages is not available today and probably never will be because he is either using you or game playing. If you really think he could be the one (even though he is being so blatantly selfish) then tell him to give you a call when he knows what he wants, has sorted himself out, and then get on with seriously dating other people. Let go of the outcome with this guy.

Mr Wonderful would never discuss ambivalent feelings with you in a way which is meant to make you hang on while he decides. Many people have ambivalent feelings early on in a relationship, but the respectful thing to do is deal with them *privately* while taking things slowly. A man may want to pull back for a little while to check out how he feels but Mr Wonderful would do this in a subtle, respectful way. He certainly wouldn't tell you his misgivings while you were lying in bed together or while you were spending a lot of time with him – that is just plain disrespectful. Accepting ambivalence will drive you into negative feelings and your vibration will plummet accordingly.

Δ Mr Controlled

This guy will ask you out, meet up with you and may even be the perfect gentleman on your date(s). He may even continue to ask and take you out but he never seems to get past first base. Here are some examples of how Mr Controlled may behave if he does get around to actually dating you:

- There are always long gaps between dates (longer than a week).
- He makes dates for a week or more in advance for no apparent reason.
- He doesn't seem to want to increase contact after the first couple of dates.
- There may be little or no communication between dates and if he does contact you it will mostly be about arrangements.
- He would never dream of calling/emailing/texting for a chat even after a couple of dates.
- He may never really seem to want to take things further sexually or to have much physical contact. (If he happily increases the physical but doesn't allow things to progress in other ways then he is more likely to be Mr Sexual or Mr Mixed Messages.)
- He may never get around to seeing you on the weekend and/or avoids important dates that arise, like Valentines.
- He may never want to spend more than a few hours with you.

What this guy seems to be saying is that he either has no time for a relationship with you or that he is not fully committed to being in one. He is unlikely to be deliberately playing games; he's more likely to be scared or cautious. Perhaps he is hoping you will take over and make the relationship happen because he doesn't want to take the risk of pursuing you and possibly being rejected. He is either more interested in being single than he realises or would prefer you to reassure him by taking the lead. While he may respond well when you nudge him, he really is not your Mr Wonderful if he is unwilling to initiate things. It's not your job to nudge or encourage men into giving you what you deserve.

What he is doing is staying in control of the emotional involvement by holding you at arms length. This is similar to Mr Mixed Messages but he restrains the emotional/sexual involvement where as Mr Mixed Messages blows hot and cold. This is confusing and frustrating for you and a sign that he is emotionally unavailable. You could have a relationship with Mr Controlled but he will use distance to control both of your feelings in the relationship – thus encouraging you to chase him.

What if he is just shy, lacking in confidence or he has been hurt before? Let me assure you: If he is so shy, lacking in confidence or hurt that has to keep you at arms length to cope, then how can he possibly be available to love you the way you deserve to be loved? His wound is making him far too self-obsessed to be able to truly consider you. Let him go and find a therapist to overcome his emotional problems rather than taking them out on you.

Mr Controlled will waste your time and end up either letting you down or annoying you – both negative feelings states that will keep you vibrating on a low level. Just don't go there. If he is your Mr Wonderful he will be more concerned with wanting to find ways to get close to you than worrying about whether or not to risk holding your hand or falling in love with you.

△ Mr Passionate

Ah, Mr Passionate! Like Mr Sexual, Mr Passionate can bowl you over with flattery and attention. The difference is that this guy is romantic and infatuated in his approach rather than overtly sexual. Apparently, you are the apple of his eye from the first date – or sometimes before you have even met. This is the man who can't stop thinking about you, calling or texting you, and who wants to see you all the time because he is just *so* into you. Or so he would like to think.

The truth is that he can't possibly be that into you until he has got to know you. He is infatuated with a fantasy or with the idea of being in love. He is not actually interested in spending time getting to know you, even if he says that he is. Mr Passionate wants to rush things and wants you to fall in love with him quickly, so he swoons over you hoping you will get caught up in his fantasy relationship. He doesn't want to go through the process of getting to know you because that would take time and be too great a risk to him. He wants a whirlwind, lots of excitement and stimulation – and you are supposed to be flattered by this and agree to feed his desires.

Mr Passionate, once ignited, is actually quite pushy and self-absorbed even though his attention appears to be on you. Like Mr Sexual, he is relating to a fantasy (and not to you as a person) so he really is not paying you any compliments, whatever nice things come out of his mouth. The worst thing about Mr Passionate is that he can be very convincing because he is *being romantic* which makes him more believable and makes you more likely to *want* to believe him. He will possibly be deluding himself as well as you, and has a very immature approach to love and relationships. The danger is that once you have fallen for this guy and got emotionally and/or sexually involved, things will often dramatically change. Once he has got you, Mr Passionate can change in any of the following ways:

- He may completely lose interest once he has got what he wants and the chase is off. This is especially the case if you sleep with him early in the relationship. He may or may not understand why this happened – some men deliberately use romance to bowl women over because it is more likely to work than overt sexual advances. On the other hand he may just be incredibly immature and not really understand why he has suddenly lost interest.

- He could turn possessive, jealous or needy if he really has become that hung up on you. Once he has secured your love, his passion can turn into the underlying neediness that it stemmed from. If his desire to 'rush things' was based on emotional insecurity then you will find that his personality or behaviour may change once he feels he has something to lose and he may end up smothering you or being possessive.

- Once he has secured your affection, he will no longer have to work at getting your attention and could turn out to be Mr Mixed Messages. It doesn't mean he will end it; he likes having a woman on the end of a string waiting for his attention. This shift could be deliberate or unconscious, but either way you could spend years waiting for his 'passion' or attention to return whilst wondering sadly what you did wrong and why he doesn't give to you any more.

This is actually a form of emotional abuse.

- Most scarily, many violent or emotionally abusive men can use displays of passion and romance at the beginning of a relationship to win their victims over. The more intense and persistent his passion, especially if he seems unable or unwilling to respect your boundaries, the more likely he is to be trying to manipulate you into going along with his desires. This man instinctively knows that once you are involved and in love with him it becomes much harder to see what's going on or to get out. This is one very good reason to be *extremely* cautious of an overly-amorous man, especially if you have a history of any sort of abuse or suffer very low self-esteem.

As with sexual attention, women can become suckers for passionate displays of interest from a man. Under this romantic influence women can lose all sense of reality and common sense, especially if they suffer low self-esteem. This is potentially the most dangerous sort of male attention because it displays a very immature and determined desire to 'get' you while *appearing* to give a woman what she really wants.

Best case scenario; he is just a bit immature in his approach but that can still lead to heartbreak when his attention suddenly trails off or he becomes possessive. Worst case scenario; he is deliberately manipulating you into becoming dependent on him so he can then abuse you. Get out *immediately* if he doesn't take no for an answer about anything to do with your personal boundaries, or if he does so begrudgingly. No matter how 'passionate' he is about you, he must show respect at all times.

Δ Mr Power Games

How is this guy different from the others? Well, this one wants it all his way and he will do whatever it takes to manipulate you into submission. He wants you, but he doesn't want to be inconvenienced or to have to make an effort for you – unless *he feels like it* and that's usually because he believes he's going to get something out of it. He wants you 'on tap' and when you aren't fully available and fitting in with his plans, he plays games to try and control you into submitting to his will. Basically, he's Mr Mixed Messages or Mr Passionate with a very nasty twist. The key thing that sets Mr Power Games apart is that he will deliberately play dirty to get his own way. It feels like you are having a game of chess with him rather than a relationship, a game that he intends to win, which of course means you have to lose. He has his own agenda and it certainly doesn't involve an equal relationship with you.

Whereas Mr Mixed Messages often doesn't realise that he is being completely selfish while he misleads you or keeps you on the end of a string, Mr Power Games can be *extremely* calculating. He will often go for strong women just so he can take pleasure in trying to control her into submission through psychological warfare. To him, love is about 'winning' and he will stoop to incredible levels to try and break you if you try to stand your ground. His main weapon is by deliberately withholding from you, especially when it's not going his way.

So what sort of thing does Mr Power Games get up to?

- If you are (genuinely) unavailable to see him when he wants to see you, he will have to retaliate in some way, often by being 'unavailable back'.
- He may be extremely casual about seeing you; for example, he may ask you out in a vague way then keep you waiting for the time and details right up until the last minute so you don't know what is happening or even if it *is* happening.
- He may expect you to just 'join in' with whatever he is doing, often hanging out with him and his friends, so you are always waiting to be alone with him.
- He may suddenly 'go off' sex or withhold affection to get your attention or to punish you because he's annoyed with you about something.
- He will often refuse to make any plans (and criticises you for wanting to) so that it is difficult for you to take care of the rest of your life, or he will change his plans at the last minute just because

he feels like it.

- He'll only do things with you that interest him, when it suits him, so you are always forced to acquiesce to his desires if you want to see him.
- He is not beyond bullying through criticism, shaming and/or verbal assaults or physical violence to put you in your place.
- He may 'disappear' literally or emotionally, often for no apparent reason, in an attempt to create abandonment fears to shake your confidence and/or get you to chase after him.
- Is frequently moody and/or aggressive, especially if he isn't getting his own way.
- He can do any of the above *without any apparent cause* just to keep you undermined and in a weaker position in the relationship.

Mr Power Games wants all the power in the relationship. If he senses that you are taking care of yourself rather than attending to his needs, he will find a way to punish you, usually through withholding or bullying, in an attempt to make you submit to him. Some of the power games he plays are very subtle; others can be overtly sexually, physically or verbally abusive. Whether he is subtle or overt; his goal is essentially the same: He wants to dominate the relationship and he does this by undermining you.

Luckily Mr Power Games will show signs very early on, even if he is behaving like a 'good guy'. One way to flush him out is to make sure that you are not too available and that you make your needs known. He won't be able to take it and will either start the tell tale 'tit for tat' games, or may even overtly criticise or shame you. When you stand your ground he will hopefully give up and move on to someone else. He can be as nice as pie if he is getting his own way, indeed he is capable of being *incredibly charming* when it suits him, but he will see you taking care of your needs as a threat to getting *his* needs met and he can turn quite aggressive. Relationships can never be equal in his eyes – it's either him or you.

This guy can be incredibly crafty, especially at the beginning, and you may find yourself being subtly undermined without even suspecting that he is game playing. The best defence against Mr Power Games is to take extremely good care of yourself *right from the beginning of a relationship* and *never* chase after a sulky or moody man.

♥ ♥ ♥

You may meet a version of Mr Unavailable who doesn't exactly fit the above descriptions or who seems like some strange hybrid mixture. Don't waste your energy trying to work out which category the guy fits into; *if he even comes close to any of the above, just disengage and stop seeing/responding to him.* If you are still not 100 percent sure, then tell him to get back to you when he has sorted 'it' out, whatever it is. A strong boundary will make him work out his priorities and help you see if he is serious about being with you.

The most important thing to remember is that Mr Wonderful is, by definition, Mr Emotionally Available. He also treats you in a *consistent and loving* manner. There are many women out there who will put up with all sorts of rubbish from a man and will assure you that you are expecting too much. Let that be their problem. If they would prefer to have Mr Unavailable than no one at all, that is their choice. If you want to manifest Mr Wonderful then you will need to invest in *much* higher standards.

There is one other thing to consider; do you recognise *yourself* in any of the descriptions about unavailable men? Do you approach relationships on a sexual level, keep decent men at arms length, give out mixed messages or bombard men because of your insecurity? These behaviours are certainly not the reserve of men! Women can and do play emotional games – they are not always the victim in a bad relationship.

If you realise that you behave like this then it may be wise to take a break from dating until you work out what is going on. If *you* are not available for a relationship then you need to take responsibility for this and consider the feelings of those you are getting involved with. Receiving attention from a man when you have no intention of committing to him is unfair and it will only serve to make you feel guilty in the end.

Getting Unhooked from Mr Unavailable

What if you are already involved with Mr Unavailable? If you don't yet feel compelled to leave, or you keep going back for more, then you still have something to 'work out' with your Self. Some call this karma; I call it *process*. For some individuals it takes a lot of work to get to the point of being able to permanently stay out of low vibration relationships, particularly if you struggled with a painful childhood.

Sometimes we are compelled to 'go there', 'stay there' or 'keep going back' in order to process something by having our buttons pressed. If you think you are in a LVR today, start taking steps to develop your relationship with yourself *despite your situation*. Don't get distracted trying to figure out if you should work it out with him or say goodbye once and for all. Instead, decide to *consciously process the relationship* rather than stick your head back in the tempting sand of denial. Read about the mental traps (below) and see if any of them apply to you. The time will come when you will know what to do and, if you have been building your self-esteem, you will also find the inner strength needed to do it.

If you are currently struggling with an ex or a 'yo-yo' relationship, then you may find the additional information on Mr Ex in the final chapter helpful. It is suggested that you read through the whole book before making decisions about any current relationship you may be engaged in. However, if you are really struggling today, you may want to skip ahead to the section on Mr Ex when you have finished reading this chapter.

Should you realise at any point that you are in a very damaging relationship or that you really can't get out, then *you will need additional support to help you gain the strength to leave.* While this book will give you many valuable insights and tools, when you are in an addictive relationship it is essential that you love yourself enough to reach out for help. *If you ask Source for help, you will be supported in your quest to heal.* I highly recommend *Women Who Love Too Much* by Robin Norwood as a starting point; however, reading books will not be enough to get you out of an addiction – action will need to be taken. Check the appendix for further suggestions and resources.

♥ *If you are involved in a low vibration relationship today, focus on developing your connection to Source, and strengthening your core self through building self-esteem and developing self loving behaviours.*

Mental Traps

Before we look at the mental traps, let's have a quick recap on some classic guises of Mr Unavailable:

- **Mr Sexual** is interested in having 'no strings' sexual attention from women.
- **Mr Non Committal** is interested in having superficial female attention without having to make any effort and/or take any real risks.
- **Mr Mixed Messages** is interested in having a woman pining over him so he can feel wanted.
- **Mr Controlled** is interested in feeling safe and will keep you at arms length to try and gain your reassurance and encouragement.
- **Mr Passionate** is interested in manipulating you into falling so fast and hard that you forget your self and give him what he wants.
- **Mr Power Games** wants to dominate you and 'win' because he believes only one person's needs can get met – at the other's expense.

When you are fed up with loving unavailable men who behave in strange or hurtful ways, it is easy to start judging them as being 'bad'. Sometimes we make these judgements to help us stay away; we wonder, if we can just convince ourselves he is really 'bad' then, perhaps, will we stop wanting him so much?

Anger is a powerful force that we sometimes use to help us get out of a low vibration relationship. While anger may help you leave, it *won't solve the problem.* Firstly, if you have to maintain an angry state to stay out of a relationship, the anger will keep you vibrating (and attracting) on a low negative level. Secondly, when the anger wears off, or he shows you his charming side, it is easy to fall back into wanting to connect with him again. This is exactly how a yo-yo relationship becomes established.

Anger and judgement don't work in the long run because deep down you know that he is a *Divine Being deserving of love.* Your soul understands that he has just forgotten who he is and feels compassion for him. No matter how awful a man's behaviour is, essentially Mr Unavailable is emotionally wounded and so it feels painful to reject him. Ultimately, we all want to love and be loved and our soul knows that anger can never lead us to the experience we desire.

Although you may well need to uncover, express and release any residue anger about being treated badly, thankfully you do not need to demonise a guy to find the strength to stay away from him. You must find the strength *within your self* and take responsibility for your relationship happiness. As well as building your self-esteem and your connection to Source, it will help if you also make sure your thoughts are free of the following mental traps:

- 'But I really love him.'
- 'But he needs me.'
- 'But he is lovely really.'
- 'But he's my soul mate.'
- 'But nobody else will want me.'

'But I really love him.'

We all know deep down that a) love will set us free (because it is the highest vibration possible) and b) that everyone is intrinsically lovable. When a woman with low self-esteem meets Mr Unavailable she intuitively knows that he needs love and that he *really is lovable* so she will set about giving him what she thinks he needs/wants, *so that he will feel loved and start being able to love her back.*

Most women have at some point loved a guy who has behaved badly and wished he could see himself the way she saw him because if he did, he wouldn't behave the way that he does and hurt her. This is perfectly natural, normal and very common. However, many women fall deeper into the trap by thinking that if they truly *love* this person then they should stay with him, *no matter what*, especially if he seems to 'need to be loved'. How can she possibly abandon him if she *loves* him?

♥ *Loving someone is not the same as having a relationship with them; you can love someone and choose not to get involved with them.*

You can love someone *absolutely* but still decide not to be with them – and this is very wise *if they are hurting you*. All too often 'love' is used as an excuse for remaining in a relationship with someone who behaves badly. 'Love' is a word that is readily banded about with pain and anguish in low vibration relationships but *love is no where to be seen*. If you choose to be with someone who hurts you, then you are choosing *not to love your self*. If you are not loving your beautiful Divine Self then you can't *possibly* be loving someone else. What you are actually doing is using them to try and fill your black hole, just as they are using you to try and fill theirs. It is mutual need that is really keeping you there.

When you are *loving* someone, you can find a way to set them free. When you are needing them, you can't – it is as simple as that. If you have to be with someone when they are hurting you or not satisfying your emotional needs, then you can't be loving them because you are unable to let them go. And if they were loving you, then they wouldn't be carelessly hurting you.

Love and need are poles apart. Yet, this is exactly what many people are doing in relationships – needing instead of loving. The first step to changing things is acknowledging that it is not love making you stay – it is need.

'But he needs me.'

Staying because we feel sorry for our lover is not a happy place to be. Staying (or getting involved) because of a sense of duty or guilt is also incredibly misguided. If you have somehow convinced yourself that the guy you are involved with can't cope without you then you are not only hurting your self, you are actually disempowering *him*.

He is an *adult* and therefore he, like you, has to take care of himself on every level. By agreeing to take care of him you are actually doing him a huge disservice: You are feeding his belief that it is your job to fill up his black hole. Let me remind you; just as no man can fill your black hole, you cannot fill any man's. Love him enough to let him find his own way home. He is far more likely to do this if you step out of the way and if he doesn't – well that's his choice and *his responsibility*.

Your focus on his needs is a projection. *You are the one who really needs you.* The degree to which you believe he needs you is the degree to which you need to connect with *your own self*. You can't help anyone when you are that disassociated from yourself. You are projecting your own need to feel loved and supported onto him. It won't help him and it certainly won't help you. Ask any woman who has been in a self-sacrificing relationship – you will never get the love you deserve from a man who 'needs' you to sacrifice *yourself* to feel ok about *himself*.

♥ *While you can't fix anyone else, you can lead by example.*

'But he is lovely really.'

They always are! If there was nothing lovely about Mr Unavailable, I doubt very much that you would be bothering. *Everyone* has a lovely side. Being lovely 99 percent of the time and only beating you up 1 percent of the time doesn't mean that he's 'lovely really', it means that he has got a serious problem which he needs to take responsibility for. If he is 'really lovely' when he is with you, but then leaves you to return home to his wife – he's not *really* being lovely to *either* of you; he is being selfish. If he's lovely when he's in a good mood and aggressive when he's not, it's the aggression that will affect you the most. You will find yourself treading on egg shells or trying to control his moods so you are safe from his verbal attacks and there's nothing lovely about that.

We fall in love with unavailable men because *we know that deep down they are lovely*. The problem is, their loveliness is tarnished by their low self-esteem and this directly affects you. They have to find a way to dig it out and share it with the woman they love and this is not more likely to happen with you putting up with their bad behaviour. In fact, it is even *less likely* because you are letting them think it is ok to treat you badly and so they won't do anything about it. Lovely or not, if he treats you badly or is unavailable in any way, he's *not lovely enough* to be involved in a relationship with you.

'But he's my soulmate.'

Ah, that old chestnut! We aren't necessarily meant to live happily ever after with our soulmate. 'soulmate' doesn't actually mean 'got to stay together'. It may mean 'got to learn to stand up for myself' or 'got to learn to love myself better' or 'got to accept reality'. If your soulmate is dangling you on a string, he may have come into your life to challenge you to cut it. Soulmates are not life sentences, they are powerful attractions to people we have met before, in another life. Sometimes they come along to prompt us to learn something. Sometimes they will be a life partner – but *only if it feels good and works well for both of you.*

♥ *If you are meant to be together, he will find a way to do the right thing by you.*

'But no one else will love me.'

This is the belief that often lies behind all the other mind traps. If we are saying this to ourselves then we are in a crippling state of low self-esteem. Staying with someone who is not right for us or getting involved with someone who treats us badly because we believe it is *all we will ever get* is an extremely painful place to be in. The sad irony is that the person you are attaching yourself to is unlikely to even love you; they are merely agreeing to stay with you because you have a mutual need. Being with someone who doesn't really love you will only make you feel worse. It is time to face and heal how you are really feeling inside.

What you are really saying is that you believe *no one will ever love you*. That is a pretty harsh statement. If you are in this feeling place today make sure you are taking the steps to raise your self-esteem suggested in this book, if you are not doing them already. Look for appropriate support outside of your relationship. Remember that you have to start by loving yourself and there is no time like the present. If you are waiting for proof that you are loved before you love your self, then you could be waiting a lifetime. Are you really willing to take that risk?

♥ ♥ ♥

There are of course many people who stumble into less than healthy relationships and manage to muddle along. The relationship may eventually improve if both partners become willing to work on it (and themselves). However, more often than not these relationships either break down or the partners learn to 'make do' with what they have, even if it means being unfaithful or chronically unhappy. If this state of affairs seems ok to you, then you are simply not ready to manifest Mr Wonderful.

♥ *You need to be 100 percent committed to creating an emotionally fulfilling relationship if you want to manifest Mr Wonderful.*

Self pity or pessimism may be completely understandable if you have been hurt, but it really won't get you what you want. If you are waiting for life to prove to you that a different kind of man exists or wants to be with you *before* you change your mind, you may end up waiting a lifetime. A change of attitude must come first and it is possible when you choose to trust the Universe and yourself. Once you are ready to change the script, focus all of your energy on lifting the cloud of negativity and freeing your most powerful manifesting tool – your mind.

If you choose to leave Mr Unavailable behind, one thing you don't need to worry about is missing out on 'the one': Mr Wonderful *is ready and willing to love you today.* You *can* attract a different sort of attention; there *are* loving men out there and they are not *all* already taken. When you are feeling discouraged, just remind yourself that you are only looking for one man and there are *millions* out there!

The Nature of Masculine and Feminine Energy

When you have decided to let Mr Unavailable go once and for all, it is time to find out how to attract the right man for you. Men and women are undeniably different when it comes to how they approach and engage in sexual relationships and it is helpful to become aware of these differences before starting to date. There is a natural flow of energy that occurs between masculinity and femininity which must be understood and respected if we are to manifest positive, fulfilling relationships with men:

1. Essentially, masculinity and femininity have equal power; their energies are complimentary but *opposite.* (That is why they are called 'opposite sexes'.)

2. Like the + and – circuit in a battery; masculinity and femininity are descriptions of a *flow of energy*, nothing more, nothing less.

3. In sexual relationships, masculine energy is naturally positive '+', forward flowing (giving) and feminine energy is naturally negative '-', drawing in (receiving). *This is precisely why they are attracted to each other.*

4. When masculine and feminine energies are free flowing they create an energetic circuit which enables Source to flow equally through *both.* The energy does not stop with the woman and nor does it truly come from the man; *It is Source Energy that flows through man to woman and is returned to Source.*

We are *all* channels for Source Energy and we can open and experience this energy in a myriad of ways. Sexual interaction (by that I mean sexual relationships, not just the sex act) is just one method of channelling Source Energy. We are living part of our Divine Purpose when we embrace our sexual nature, which is based on the attraction and connection of polar opposites: masculinity and femininity. (Same sex relationships also have this flow of positive/negative energy. Sexuality is *essentially* the coming together of masculine/feminine opposites.)

An Energetic Role Reversal

When suffering from low self-esteem, both men and women energetically reverse or block this natural flow of energy in their relationships. Women with low self-esteem give too much and/or refuse to receive; men with low-self esteem expect to be given to and/or refuse to give. In an unhealthy relationship, the woman often ends up energetically *flowing toward the man* and the man often *expects to be emotionally 'filled' by the woman.*

A woman with LSE (low self-esteem) feels she must *give more* love to a man to make him want to love her back. A man with LSE expects a doting woman to *take responsibility for making him feel better* about himself, believing one day he will find something in himself to give to her. A woman with LSE believes she has to *earn* love and a man believes he has to be *loved more.* The energy flow gets blocked because the woman's natural ability to be wooed has been wounded and the man's natural ability to pursue and offer a woman love is damaged.

When a man feels good about himself he *wants* to share what he has with the woman he loves. He wants to pursue her, woo her, impress her and make her feel special. When she is happy around him, he feels proud that he has been able to contribute to her happiness which in turn makes him feel emotionally fulfilled. *Nothing pleases a man more than being able to make the woman he loves happy.*

When he feels unsure of his own worth, he questions his masculinity and his ability to provide for a woman's needs. Because a man with low self-esteem doubts his ability to win the love of a woman he may end up playing emotional games or engaging in fantasy relationships instead. If he goes beyond fantasy and actually dates women, he will either try to manipulate her into wanting to give to *him*, or dominate and bully her into staying and 'loving' him the way he thinks he should be loved. Abusive men try to force love out of women rather than winning it because they feel inadequate.

Even if a man manages to trick or force a woman into emotional involvement – it will never solve his feelings of low self-esteem; it will only make him secretly feel bad about himself for the way he is behaving and angry with her for allowing him to behave badly. Some men with LSE opt out altogether by chasing women who are completely out of reach, thus making the flow of masculine/feminine energy impossible.

A man operating on a low vibration will be attracted to his energetic counterpart – a woman with low self-esteem *who expects to have to give an endless supply of love in order to be tolerated*, or a woman who expects to be dominated by a bully. She expects to have to work at making *him* feel loved because she feels guilt or shame about having any needs herself. If a woman has cripplingly low self-esteem, her pain can be so powerful that it drive her to stay with a man who abuses her physically, sexually and/or emotionally in an effort to try and 'earn' his love. This is really sad, especially when you realise that he should be the one trying to win *her* love.

A woman's natural 'feminine' state is one of receiving the determined, genuine, loving interest of a man. She is the prize and her love must be won by her suitor because *she is the Goddess incarnate*: a physical manifestation of the feminine because she is endowed with the gift of life. She is precious *just because she is a woman*. Men with high self-esteem are naturally drawn to wanting to capture a part of the feminine for themselves, to secure a relationship with a woman they can adore and protect.

If a man manages to woo and capture his love by making her feel happy and secure with him, he will have fulfilled his sexual mission.

Feminine energy is *supposed* to be sought and secured by masculine energy. Women are *supposed* to be pursued, wooed and 'captured' by men. And when it is done with love and honour, *both will feel emotionally fulfilled.*

Does this mean that a woman should never give to a man or that men should never receive from a woman? Of course not! We are not talking in absolute terms here; we are talking about the basic principles of an *energy flow.* What I am suggesting is that women who have low-self esteem tend to take on the masculine principle of *flowing forward* (towards the man) and that a man with low self-esteem tends to take on the feminine principle of expecting to receive from the woman.

When Women Give Too Much

When a woman feels good about herself, she knows she is special and worthy of a man's love *just as she is.* The self-doubting woman doesn't want to risk waiting for a wonderful guy because *she doesn't believe he will try to find her or won't want her if he does find her.* So she looks for a man who seems to *need* her. If he has almost nothing to offer her, she consoles herself with the fact that at least he is unlikely to leave her. And she convinces herself that if she works hard enough at giving him her 'love', maybe one day he will have something to give back.

Interestingly, this role reversal mimics the mother-son relationship where the energy naturally flows the other way – from mother to child. When a woman is emotionally mature she is able to receive and to take care of her needs as well as to give. She instinctively knows that *it makes her more effective as a carer if her needs are also met.* She also knows that she deserves consideration. A woman receives from a man *not because she can't do without male input,* but because she will feel much better and be more able to give when some of her needs are also taken care of by the man who loves her.

Men 'take care' of women not because women can't cope on their own, but because men also need to feel needed and useful in the mating dance. They not only desire the right to be by a woman's side but they also want to feel they can contribute to caring for their young by caring for their children's mother who births and feeds them. (This impulse is present whether or not a couple decide to have children.)

When women feel emotionally deprived they often become overly 'motherly' and focus on meeting everyone else's needs and ignoring their own, hoping one day someone will notice their sacrifices and want to meet *their* needs. When men feel emotionally deprived they often want someone to 'mother' them, give them what they feel is missing and enable them to reach what they believe is an elusive masculine self-esteem. What a man *actually* needs to come into his power is to have his masculine desire activated.

If a woman flows toward a man to try and fill him up *she only makes him feel more impotent*, even if he tells her that this is what he needs or expects. Somewhere inside him is the instinct to try and mate with a woman he finds special. When he finds her, his desire to be with her will ignite his passions like nothing else. The male desire to join with woman is incredibly powerful, far more powerful than his desire to be mothered. And when he falls in love with a woman and she makes him work to win her love, he will find unexpected reserves of instinctive male self-esteem which is, after all, designed to keep the species going! Motherly encouragement, support and hyper-availability will only take the wind out of his sails.

♥ *Sexual desire is what triggers a man's innate masculine power.*

You can do nothing about a man's low self-esteem; he has to find his own way to deal with it. And because you can never fix it for him, getting involved with a needy man is never going to lead you to the love you seek; it will only serve to lower your vibration. If a man is refusing to make an effort or has nothing to offer you *it is not a reflection of how lovable you are, it is a reflection of how low his self-esteem is or that you are simply not the right woman for him* – that is all. And if you should decide to get involved with a man to try to fix him this is not a reflection of how much you love him, it is a reflection of *your* low self-esteem – which of course you *can* do something about!

♥ *You are the Goddess incarnate and you deserve to be cherished by a man.*

This is in no way meant to suggest that men are inferior to women. Men and women are equal. *All* human beings are equal. However, the flow of Source Energy requires masculinity to be mysteriously and powerfully drawn to the feminine so they can merge and potentially create life. Think about the sperm and the egg: The egg, once it is released, floats down into the uterus giving off signals that she is ready to 'receive' a sperm. All the sperm actively and eagerly swim towards the egg, searching her out in an effort to win the chance to join with her. Each sperm competes with all the others to be 'chosen' to merge and start new life. Any sperm that goes around in circles or can't get it together doesn't stand a chance. Now, can you imagine an egg chasing sperm in an effort to get one of them to take a bite? Never in a million years!

When Women Refuse To Receive

As part of our collective spiritual development, we have gone through a dark period where the male principle of 'giving' has been used to justify the universal male control of women. Anyone can see that *true giving has absolutely nothing to do with control.* However, if the recipient (woman) apparently *needs* what the giver (man) has to give, the giver holds a power over the receiver. It has been believed for millennia that women *need* men, not only to fulfil their roles as women but to survive. Because of this collective belief, *all human social structures have been created in a way which made it impossible for women to operate outside of the control of male authority.* In the 20th Century, feminists were busy proving that women *do not need men* and therefore do not have to accept male authority or superiority.

♥ *The very foundations of Western society have been dramatically transformed because women are free to make their own life and relationship choices.*

This shift in social structures has left men and women unsure about how to relate to each other, especially when it comes to dating and marriage:

> Women can say, 'I can live without you thanks.'
> So men say, 'I don't know what women want from me any more.'
> Women can say, 'I don't need you to take care of me.'
> So men say, 'I can never make her happy.'
> Women can say, 'If you don't buck up I am leaving you.'
> So men say, 'I don't see the point in making an effort anymore.'

We are in a position, perhaps for the first time in recorded history, where women can make their own choices and think for themselves instead of being entirely governed by external (male governed) social structures. What makes things even more challenging is that we are bombarded with constant media messages that change with the wind and often contradict themselves. It is extremely confusing for all concerned.

Despite the fact that women have categorically said that they want more from their relationships, many haven't got a clue how to actually *receive* from a man. Traditionally, receiving from men has been laced with the poison of dependency and loss of control, so women are understandably nervous about how to receive in a fulfilling way. Many women are terrified that if they open themselves to receiving from a man they may find themselves dependent and weakened again. Thankfully, when men and women have high self-esteem they find that they are able to create equal, loving relationships which are *also* open to the natural flow of Divine Masculine/Feminine Energy.

Now that we know that women don't need men to survive or even to fulfil our roles as mothers, we can pluck from the rubble of former social structures that which is valuable and true: *masculinity is forward flowing and femininity is receiving*. Remembering this will enable us to form a new way for men and women to relate to each other *which works for both parties.*

♥ *We must begin our journey from the fundamental premise that a woman enters into a relationship with a man through choice, not necessity.*

From this position of strength and empowerment women can also accept that, because of the nature of the Divine Masculine/Feminine Energies, a woman *does need to be open to receive from a man if she wants to be in a happy sexual relationship with him.* Equally, a man must be willing and able to give to the woman he loves if he is ever going to find happiness with her.

♥ *In a healthy relationship dance between a man and a woman, essentially the man gives (flows forward) and the woman receives.*

Trusting the Masculine Desire to Pursue and Capture

Today there is very little 'love and honour' in the dating game. Courting in our culture has all but died a death, except perhaps in romantic comedies. The social morals which forced a man to court a woman and ask her to marry him before he could enjoy the fruits of his labour have been destroyed in women's (rightful) plight to have control of our own bodies and relationships.

As a result of this many 'liberated' women readily give their love and bodies as if they are as valuable as an old pair of jeans. The idea of 'free love' was born in the 60's and despite what popular culture suggests, for men this has been an absolute disaster because love that is 'free' *becomes worthless.* Just because men are seemingly happy indulging in 'free love' (love and sex that requires little or no effort on their part), it doesn't mean that they haven't also become disillusioned and confused by the turn of events.

The masculine drive to *pursue and capture the woman he believes is worth his effort* has been short-circuited by women's hyper availability and apparent lack of self-worth. If women don't value them selves how can men value and desire them? And if men can no longer find a woman to value, they have absolutely no reason to make an effort. When men lose their desire to win women over, they become deeply dissatisfied, *even if they are getting 'free' sex every night.* This is because the essential motivating ingredient in the mating ritual has been lost.

Despite what society implies – easy access to sex or a sexual relationship doesn't fire masculine passions in the way that the challenge of winning a woman over does. After the initial novelty wears off, they usually lose their interest and their desire, even if they continue to indulge in casual sex or decide to conveniently stay with the woman they didn't have to work at capturing. Casual sex can become addictive when a man wonders if perhaps he feels unsatisfied because he is not getting 'enough' or women aren't 'sexy enough'. He may feel the need to look for more sex when what is really missing is a woman who is truly precious to him.

A man likes to have 'goals' to score (finding a woman to pursue, scoring the first date, the first kiss, getting her agreement to see him exclusively, to spend the night with him, to marry him and spend her life with him, to bear *his* children rather than some other guy's.) What makes a man feel really good is being able to strive and reach these goals without the woman prompting, pre-empting or handing herself over to him before he has even asked.

♥ *If capturing a woman is too easy it won't really mean anything to a man and he may not even know why.*

Men like to feel gentle resistance from the woman they are pursuing, *so he can feel he has done a good job when he finally wins her over.* He wants to feel like it was all his idea and that *she's worth all the effort.* Men with high self-esteem also enjoy some healthy competition from other potential suitors because he likes to know that he has won the affection of the woman he loves *despite* the competition. He wants to feel that *she has chosen him above all others* and that she hasn't handed herself over to him on a plate and begged him to eat.

For a woman to become choosey *she has to feel valuable and worthy in herself.* If she throws herself at the first man who shows an interest, or worse still at a man who has shown *no* interest – she obviously is not being choosey at all and he won't have to make any effort to win her love. He may well go ahead and take advantage of what is offered, but his passions won't be ignited in a lasting way and they will *both* feel cheated.

Women need to find a way to transform and internalise the old social structures which acted as a sexual barrier by learning to *value our beautiful selves.* We need to replace those external structures with new internal boundaries. The old structures shamed women into living and behaving in a certain way. We need to be grown-ups who take responsibility for creating our own boundaries instead of relying on society to tell us how to act.

Although men pursue women, it is women who collectively lead the mating dance. By valuing ourselves and being choosey about sharing our love and our sacred bodies we give men something to work for. Men respond positively by actively pursuing women who value themselves because they want to merge with the Goddess: the Divine Feminine that resides in womankind.

♥ *A valuable woman is a woman who has remembered who she is.*

Becoming Choosey
In the same way that sperm are driven to want to join with the egg, what (heterosexual) men want most is to win the chance to join with the Goddess incarnate – to find a woman who is special to him.

♥ *When a man is finally 'chosen' by a woman after all his efforts he feels special and worthy because he has successfully reached his desired masculine goal.*

How to Become Choosey:
1. *Never, ever* actively chase after a man
2. Stop trying to encourage men to love you by *giving* to them
3. Stop jumping through hoops to be with a man

4. Stop trying to 'mother him' or 'love him better'
5. Stop giving in too quickly or easily to a man's advances
6. Don't try to persuade him to swim toward you
7. Don't despair if a man doesn't make the grade and you have to let him go

1. *Never, ever* actively chase after a man

Eggs don't chase sperm!

2. Stop trying to encourage men to love you by giving to them

He wants the chance to win you with *his* offerings and efforts and you need to know he has something to offer you. It will more than satisfy him just to know that he can make you happy. If you give to him you are telling him that you are trying to win *his* love. It is impossible to be choosey whilst you are desperately trying to earn a man's love. Instead you give out the message that you do not value your self.

3. Stop jumping through hoops to be with a man

Sperm jump through hoops to get to the egg. The egg waits to see which sperm deserves the big prize! It is not 50/50 when it comes to men dating women. He *must* be driven to come to her. She must be patient and *choosey*. And being choosey is very different from being passive. (You are being passive when you decide to only accept whatever crumbs you are offered.)

4. Stop trying to 'mother him' or 'love him better'

This will only decrease his desire and squelch his motivation to work at winning your love *because it infantilises him*. It will also make you resentful over time when he doesn't give you what you want in return. (And believe me; a man will *never* give you what you want if he is happy for you to mother him.) The best way to motivate a man is by showing him you are valuable (choosey). The best way to support a man is by *believing in him*. Agreeing to or insisting on trying to meet his 'needs' tells him he is a boy in your eyes and not up to the job of being your royal consort.

5. Stop giving in too quickly or easily to a man's advances

Allow him work a little for your attention. This is *not* about playing games. Game playing is attempting to undermine someone so you can get one over them. When you are choosey (not so easily won over) you actually *empower* the right guy to rise to the occasion. When a man does the same to a woman, he *is* trying to disempower her because he doesn't feel he is up to the job of winning her love by impressing her. So, instead he is tries to capture her by undermining or tricking her. This is the difference between men and women: masculinity flows toward femininity; men chase women; women become valuable by being choosey. A woman with high self-esteem wants to check a suitor is worthy of her time and energy *before* she gets emotionally involved and a man needs to feel he has successfully won his woman over. It is a win-win situation when you hold back a little.

6. Don't try to persuade him to swim toward you

At each new stage in the relationship, *allowing him to ask you* makes him feel he is slowly gaining your trust and winning you over. He treats relationship milestones like personal goals and he likes to feel *he has achieved them* when he successfully gets you to agree to do them with him. When you ask/badger him *you are 'chasing the sperm' rather than being choosey*! Besides, you need to know that he *really* wants to take it to the next stage, that he is not just going along with you because it is easy or convenient or until someone better comes along. When a man finds the courage to ask you for something – *you know he really wants it. You* are the one who should be saying yea or nay to his requests for a date, a kiss, a weekend away, or your hand in marriage, not the other way around. This makes *you* choosey and the *right man* want you more.

7. Don't despair if a man doesn't make the grade and you have to let him go

Remember *you are the Goddess incarnate*. There are plenty more sperm in the sea willing to seek you out. There is no use lamenting over a sperm that swims in circles or can't be bothered to swim toward you at all. The egg is *far* too dignified to be worrying about that. Remember, you are only looking for *one* Mr Wonderful. All the others just aren't him – so move on!

♥ ♥ ♥

If a man can't find the desire to pursue and treat you well, it is because:

1. It is not the right time for him to have a relationship (he's just dabbling or has personal issues to work through).
2. He hasn't found the right woman yet.
3. His partner is (inadvertently) taking the wind out of his sails.

♥ *The only part in a man's desire you have any control of is whether or not you are taking the wind out of his sails.*

When a man really desires a woman he will be motivated to do what it takes to win her love and secure her attention *over an extended period of time*. When a man is ready to love he will be on the lookout for a special woman. Sometimes he will even be caught off guard when he *isn't* looking. He will think a woman is special when he finds her attractive and when he believes that she is valuable. Together these ingredients will ignite his desire to win her love and if he is really interested in her, you can rest assured that he won't give up easily. The more effort he has to make, the more valuable he will think the woman is.

All you can do to increase the chances of a man you like pursuing you is make sure you are not taking the wind out of his sails. The best way to avoid this happening is to *value yourself as the Goddess that you are and allow him the opportunity to win you over.*

Δ Women take the wind out of a man's sails by:
1. Reversing the flow of m/f energy

2. Being hyper-available to him
3. Refusing to receive from him

Δ Women *reverse the flow* of m/f energy when it comes to dating by:

- Answering men's personal ads
- Introducing themselves to men they are interested in
- Asking men out on dates
- Phoning/texting/emailing men who have not contacted them first
- Telling a man where/when to meet them for a date
- Paying the bill on a date
- Offering sex before he has shown an interest in it
- Asking/suggesting to live together
- Asking him if he wants to get married

Δ Women make themselves 'hyper-available' by:

- Replying instantly to emails/texts/phone calls or using MSN
- Accepting last minute dates (less than three days notice at the beginning).
- Seeing him more than twice a week during the first few weeks
- Allowing him into their home before they dated at least three times
- Agreeing to sex (anything but kissing) before the relationship is exclusive
- Agreeing to an exclusive relationship before going on at least six dates
- Agreeing to 'hang out' with him and/or his friends before the relationship is well established
- Saying 'I love you' before he does
- Leaving overnight things at his house, especially uninvited
- Moving into his house or allowing him to move into yours before you are making plans to get married (unless you have both categorically agreed that you will not get married).
- Giving him the key to their home or accepting his before it is agreed that you are getting married or moving in together.

Δ Women refuse to receive from men by:

- Not letting him pay on a date
- Refusing to allow him to open doors or engage in other chivalrous acts
- Not allowing a man to fix things or help
- Saying no to a man escorting you home or picking you up to go out (unless you have not yet met him and it is for safety reasons)
- Not letting him drive; insisting on driving instead
- Rebuffing any of his compliments
- Refusing his gifts or insisting on 'paying him back'

If you indulge in any of the above, you are going to have to change your dating habits! If a guy really loves you, the odd slip is unlikely to scare him instantaneously. However, if you do any of the above you are at serious risk of taking the wind out of his sails now or as your relationship progresses. The best policy is to start as you mean to continue.

When you do any of the above you are basically saying that you don't trust that a man will love you properly and that you don't deserve such consideration. It's time to trust that you are valuable and worth pursuing. It's also time to trust that the right man will *want* to care for you. I am not suggesting you become 'passive' – far from it. I am reminding you that being *choosey* is both self-affirming *and* attractive to Mr Wonderful; being choosey is the absolute opposite of being passive. Actively receiving from a man keeps the love energy flowing and makes you *both* feel good.

The Characteristics of Mr Wonderful

So far in this chapter we have been looking at the sort of negative male attention and female behaviour that lowers your vibration. We have also looked at some of the mental traps that may encourage you to engage with Mr Unavailable and the difference between masculine and feminine energies. Now let's put the picture together and look more closely at Mr Wonderful and how he would behave.

Essentially 'Mr Wonderful' is any man you could have a wonderful relationship with. He is vibrating on a reasonable level so he is able to give you what you are looking for. He is not perfect but he is emotionally *available* because he has a reasonable degree of self-esteem and most essentially, he wants *you*.

Mr Wonderful:

- Finds you attractive *and* is interested in you as a person
- Would choose his life partner based on more than sexual attraction alone
- Makes you feel good because he is respectful and concerned with your happiness and comfort; he is thinking about *you* not his sexual appetite
- Shows his appreciation for you by paying you a (non sexual) compliment or by asking you out
- Is busy thinking about what he needs to do to make you feel comfortable and relaxed in his company rather than worrying about whether or not to ask you out or hold to your hand
- Is happy to pursue a relationship with you and will enable things to progress slowly and calmly
- Is available and ready to love you *today* (He would wait until he was ready before approaching you, out of respect for your feelings)
- May pull back for a little while to check out how he feels but he does so in a *gentle and respectful* way
- Deals with any challenging feelings he has about getting involved *privately*
- Takes things slowly so he can check out how he feels about you and is keen for you to get to know him
- Respects your boundaries and does his best to consider your needs and feelings at all times
- Is willing to take reasonable risks in order to woo you and win your love
- Wants to gradually spend more time with you, have contact with you between dates and finds ways to share his life with you

- Is consistent, reliable and takes responsibility for making you feel cared for
- Loves to make an effort for you
- Enjoys taking care of your needs as best he can
- Sees his relationship with you as a mutual and equal exchange of love

Doesn't that sound more like it? Doesn't he sound *wonderful*? I don't know about you, but just reading this list makes me give a sigh of relief and feel more relaxed about the idea of being in a relationship. Mr Wonderful has high self-esteem. Mr Wonderful has something to offer and he wants to share it with *you*.

♥ How to Use the List of Mr Wonderful's Characteristics:

1. Know that nothing on the above list is negotiable
2. Know that when you first start dating a man you will not know who he is
3. Know that just because a man has asked you out and you find him attractive does not make him 'Mr Wonderful until proved otherwise'

1. Know that here is absolutely nothing on the above list which is negotiable

If you meet a man and he does not possess *all* of the above qualities – you can be sure that he's not *your* Mr Wonderful. He may not be ready to get involved yet or he may 'just not be that into you'. Either way, it is not your job to try and get whatever is missing out of him or to encourage him to come up with the goods; it is your job to make sure *you are being choosey*. Once you have let a guy into your life and/or your body it becomes *much* harder to get him out again. Women are supposed to be choosey and slow to be 'won over' so you can emotionally protect yourself.

2. Know that when you first start dating a man you will not know who he is

Even if you have known a guy for *years*, until you are actually dating him, you won't know how he is going to treat you in a committed relationship. It is important to take your time getting to know him *as a suitor* before you become lovers. Date him before becoming exclusive with him. It is important that he shows that he is willing to make the effort to woo you before you get sexually involved with him. Be sure that you can happily tick *everything* on the above list before you decide he is Mr Wonderful. And give yourself time to find out.

3. Know that just because a man has asked you out and you find him attractive does not make him 'Mr Wonderful until proved otherwise'

He is merely a potential suitor vying for your attention and *that is all.* While it is great to have a suitor vying for your attention, women with LSE are prone to leaping to conclusions because they can't believe their luck; an attractive man has actually asked them out and suddenly that is all that matters! If you think like this you put yourself in an extremely vulnerable position and you are very likely to get hurt sooner or later. You need to become blasé about suitors, even if you think one is the hottest thing since Johnny Depp. He is simply 'Mr Interested' *until he has proven* that he is also your Mr Wonderful.

Chapter 5

Planting

Working the Magic

How Do You Tell the Universe What You Want?

Manifesting is an art. The key to developing the art of manifesting is to understand and *utilise* the Law of Attraction. So, before we continue, let's recap on the basic principles and how we apply them.

♥ The 12 Principles of the Law of Attraction:

1. The Law of Attraction works on an *energetic* level.
2. *Everything* is energy, including the body you inhabit. Your thoughts and especially *the feelings attached to them* are energy.
3. Energy vibrates at different levels and frequencies: positive = higher: negative = lower.
4. Energy is *always* attracted to other energy vibrating on the same frequency – like attracts like, positive attracts positive and negative attracts negative.
5. Your most frequent thoughts *and the feelings that are attached to them* will at some point manifest in physical reality: You are continually co-creating your own reality through your thoughts and *the feelings attached to them.*
6. If you are thinking *and feeling* positively, it automatically follows that you will attract positive manifestations into your life.
7. Thoughts with strong feelings attached to them are *extremely powerful energy vibrations* and our thoughts will manifest things which are a vibrational match; things that are vibrating on the same frequency (or level).
8. Our part in the co-creation of what comes into our life is in *sending out the thought/feeling energy.* The Universe responds by bringing

us what we have 'asked' for through our choice of energy vibration. If we *ask* for positive by *sending out* positive then we will be *sent* positive in response.

9. When we are sent something *we can choose whether or not we want to receive* it.

10. Responding to something we don't want in a negative way will not make it go away. *It will make it stay or attract more of the same* because we are sending out more negative to the Universe, apparently asking for more negativity to be sent.

11. A conscious person can choose to *transform the negative 'don't want' into a positive 'do want'* and vibrate it back out to the Universe in order to change a manifestation.

12. You can change your life with the power of positive thoughts/feelings as long *as you are not too attached to a specific outcome*. Attachment is fear – fear is negative – and negativity will only attract more negative manifestations. Openness to what the Universe will deliver is therefore absolutely essential to positive manifestations.

Principles 1-8 of the Law of Attraction relate to raising your vibration (self-esteem) by connecting to Source Energy and actively loving your self. *Changing the way you feel* is the single most important principle in the book because it will automatically raise your energy vibration. It usually won't happen overnight, but without a doubt it *will* happen and it will make a huge difference in all areas of your life. The more you work at this, the better the results will be.

When we work with Principles 9, 10 and 11 we realise that once we are connected to Source, we can further raise our vibration by learning to *change the way we respond to negative mirrors* and by consciously focusing our emotional energy on what we *do* want. We can accept that while we are not perfect, we *are* intrinsically valuable and we do not need to 'internalise' any negative mirrors that appear in our lives; we can learn to simply say 'no thanks' and walk away. In relationships with men we also learn to recognise the many faces of 'Mr Unavailable' in order to strengthen our ability to promptly decline these negative mirrors and to send out a message about what we *are* looking for. In the next stage of the journey we will be developing our understanding of Principle 12 and learning how to apply it.

Principle 12: You can change your life with the power of positive thoughts/feelings as long *as you are not too attached to a specific outcome*. Attachment is fear – fear is negative – and negative will attract more negative. Openness to what the Universe will deliver is therefore absolutely essential to positive manifestations.

♥ *In the beginning of a relationship the best way to make sure you do not become 'too attached' to a specific outcome is to become blasé about dating.*

The Dating Game

If you have been working hard to raise your vibration, develop a strong core self, and transform the way you view sexual relationships with men, then you have already taken great strides in the right direction. So what now? Do you say a magic spell and sit back to wait for your special delivery to arrive?

The question about the role of the Universe in delivering a 'decent' man has haunted me on my journey – I have struggled with it on many occasions. I have read many dating books which *all* encourage being proactive and 'getting yourself out there' to improve your chances of meeting someone special. However, when you read books on manifesting they assure the reader that all you need to do to manifest is *send your (positive) intentions out and let the Universe do the rest.*

Despite my many attempts at manifesting, no wonderful man ever arrived in the mail, so to speak, and this confused me. I wondered if perhaps the dating books were right; maybe I did have to *help the Universe bring me a man* by going out there and finding him myself or by making myself 'more available'?

The problem with this thinking, of which I have always been uncomfortably aware, is that it shows a lack of trust in the Universe and in the feminine qualities of attraction. I have manifested other things (including jobs and places to live) without any effort at all – so why would I have to work *really hard* to get the Universe to bring me Mr Wonderful? I asked myself; *shouldn't the guy be the one who jumps through hoops to find me?*

At one point I even dared myself to simply stop looking for a relationship – to stop doing *anything* to help me meet men. I dared myself to hand it *all* over to the Universe, to just stop *trying* altogether. I realised very quickly that this filled me with utter dread. *What if he misses me? What if he can't find me? What if I do have to be out there 'making myself available'?* I was reminded of my deep fear that if I didn't bend over backwards to encourage a man and let him know that I was interested he just wouldn't bother with me. It brought me face to face with my crippling belief that I have to *earn* love: that I have to *work at* being noticed and wanted by men. The fear of not being 'found' or 'noticed' pressed some very painful buttons.

♥ *'Getting out there' to meet men in an attempt to make sure you don't 'miss the boat' is really not a positive, self affirming reason.*

While part of me has always been truly convinced that the Universe would bring a relationship without any effort on my part, the other stronger part was terrified that if I didn't keep 'trying', a good relationship would just pass me by. So, I was left wondering how manifesting applies to relationships – do you learn to love yourself then wait for a knock at the door or for a stranger on a bus to ask you out? If you are not being 'pro-active' about meeting men, won't Mr Wonderful be unable to find you, and the Universe unable to deliver?

The Universe doesn't need a helping hand from you in bringing your special delivery, but there is another very good reason to 'get out there' and meet men. If you have been doing the essential inner work then the Universe will find a way to somehow bring him to you; you really don't need to worry about how and when, you just need to trust.

You already know that you can either help or hinder the Universe in meeting your request through *your vibration* and your response to negative mirrors. Aside from that, you do not need to 'help' the Universe to make it happen. However, you *do* need to be pro-active when it comes to dating, not to help the Universe but to help you.

You need to help *yourself* become more able to both recognise and receive Mr Wonderful when he appears. You need to become blasé about dating men to avoid scaring off Mr Wonderful by taking the wind out of his sails or by getting caught up with Mr Unavailable because you *can't believe your luck* when someone shows an interest in you. In order to be able to practice dating skills, you need to meet men – *lots* of men. And you won't meet lots of men while you are sitting at home waiting for the special delivery to arrive!

♥ *The best way to prepare for receiving Mr Wonderful is to practice your dating skills.*

If you are anything like I was at the beginning of my process, you will have a long way to go in being able to successfully deal with Mr Unavailable. Well, don't worry; the Universe will happily provide you with *plenty* of opportunities to practice once you get out there!

You *could* choose to sit at home working on your self-esteem and practice raising your vibration, send your intention to the Universe and then wait. There really is absolutely nothing stopping you from doing this, but if you have been vibrating on a low level and attracting men on the emotional bottom rung, you will still have to demonstrate to the Universe (and yourself) that you are moving up the vibrational relationship ladder. You are highly unlikely to make one huge leap from 'alcoholic' or 'womaniser' to a relationship with Mr Wonderful without practising *your own* new behaviours. Meeting men will, at the very least, give you this essential practice.

Remember, manifesting a loving relationship is not the same as manifesting a nice new dress or a sum of money. Many of us have incredibly entrenched behaviour and belief systems which we have to work hard at changing, *especially when it comes to sexual relationships*. If you are ready to be loved the way you want to be loved it won't take much practice at all and Mr Wonderful is probably already on his way. If, however, you have years of self-defeating habits and entrenched negative beliefs, then it may take *a lot* of practice and you must be willing to put in the leg work.

When you practice dating you are ploughing the field and sowing the seeds. You are not helping the Universe to bring Mr Wonderful to you because the Universe doesn't need your help. Nor are you working hard to 'earn the right' to be loved – you are loveable just as you are. *You are simply helping yourself become more ready to receive love.* By practising dating you will gradually raise your vibration through practising the art of becoming choosey.

You will need to keep practising until you *are* choosey, until you have internalised the belief that you deserve the best treatment from a man and it is second nature to say 'no thanks' to Mr Unavailable. If you are anything like me, you will have to say 'no thanks' to more than a handful of men before you really get it. Each time you do it, *it will become easier* and you will grow more aware that you are indeed the Goddess incarnate.

♥ *If you want a relationship with Mr Wonderful you first have to become an expert at recognising and declining Mr Unavailable.*

Dating men will help you become ready for the relationship you want because *the Universe will send you all the men you need to practice dealing with all your little weaknesses that undermine you getting the love you deserve.* If you have a penchant for attached men, you can be sure the Universe will send married men until you get over it. If you are a sucker for alcoholics, you'll get one seemingly charming offer after another... until you learn to say 'no thanks'. If you get caught out by men who love to get you to chase them, you'll get dangling carrots galore until you learn stop gazing at those carrots with a longing heart. And guess what?

♥ *The more men you date, the more immune to Mr Unavailable you become because dating lots of men makes you blasé.*

If you have had nothing romantic happen for five years and then some guy shows an interest in you – you will be tempted to sweep his 'short comings' (unavailability) under the carpet because *you can't believe your luck*. If you were already dating three other men, it is highly unlikely that you would be quite so bowled over by his attention. You would really *know* that there are plenty more fish in the sea... because you are dating them!

While you are practising dating you will also be refining your request for Mr Wonderful to the Universe. Every time you say 'no thanks' to Mr Unavailable and spend time turning those 'don't wants' into 'do wants', you are sending the Universe a strong message *which has added emotional potency*. Another advantage to practising dating is that you will also automatically feel less needy and this will raise your vibration and make it easier to attract what you do want. Sitting at home waiting for a knock at the door will simply not allow you to grow in this way.

When you focus all your attention on raising your vibration by becoming blasé (unattached) and choosey, you can be sure that the Universe will take care of the rest. Trust that the Universe will send you whatever you need, whenever you need it, because its job is to help you in your noble quest.

♥ *Manifesting a loving relationship is a deep inner process not an instant magic trick.*

Becoming Blasé about Dating

Becoming blasé about dating men will *enable you to become choosey*. Being choosey will both raise your vibration *and* make you more attractive to the right man. It is impossible to be choosey if you care about the outcome with every suitor or get hung up on a particular man before he has committed to you. The only thing you should be caring about is whether or not you save your emotional investment for when you know you have Mr Wonderful wooing you. Remaining 'unattached to the outcome' does not mean not caring about how things turn out; it means not getting caught up on the details of how and when Mr Wonderful will arrive.

The Universe is already working on your behalf because you have been making changes and therefore showing your intentions. Do not concern yourself with the details of how the Universe will provide for you, trust that it is already doing so and *the timing will be perfect.*

♥ *Before you begin dating make sure you are ready.*

If you know you are not emotionally available for a relationship it is not fair to put yourself out there for men to ask you out. You need to be honest with yourself. If it has been some time since you did the assessment, have another go and see if there have been any changes. Any man you meet while you are mending your relationship with yourself can wait – and he will wait if he is genuinely interested. If you have therapy to do, a relationship to get out of, or an addiction to kick – *deal with that first.* If you are still discovering who you are and what is important to you, then give yourself the time you need. There really is no hurry. This is a process, not a race.

Once you feel ready, take it slowly and make sure you are fully prepared. Finish reading this book and do more dating research if you feel you need to. Have a plan so you do not get overwhelmed. Dating can be hard work, especially if you are also trying to change entrenched habits or beliefs.

I don't want to put you off because dating can be great fun and can be really rewarding, especially once you realise you are beginning to make progress. But when you are starting out and making mistakes it pays to be prepared so you don't give up at the first hurdle and you don't let any disappointments slow you down. The good news is, the more blasé you become, the less disappointed you will feel if it things don't work out with a suitor!

♥ How to Become Blasé About Dating:

1. Keep raising your self-esteem
2. Keep the rest of your life
3. Date lots of men
4. Put up an ad or join an agency
5. Keep your options open
6. Don't count your chickens
7. Don't get sexually involved until he has successfully won you over
8. Don't consider him serious until he has asked you out at least six times
9. Don't consider it a relationship until it is exclusive
10. Create some real hurdles for him to get to you

1. Keep raising your self-esteem

Before we get into the details of the dating game it is worth reminding you that if you scored low on self-esteem, *you must continue focusing on raising it*. Dating is not a substitute for connecting with Source Energy, having a relationship with your self or raising your vibration by developing your self-esteem. On the contrary, dating will almost certainly cause a less-than-solid core self to wobble and it is important that you take this into consideration. You don't need perfect self-esteem to date but this process requires you to at least be working toward discovering that you are worthy of love. The higher your self-esteem, the easier it will be to become blasé, so keep at it.

2. Keep the rest of your life

If you believe the only thing worth having in life is a relationship, then your life is bound to feel empty and pointless without one. Not only will this thinking lower your vibration, it will make it impossible to be blasé about dating. If you think that a relationship is all that counts, then it puts you under a lot of pressure to 'get' one. This is hardly being 'choosey'!

A love relationship is only *one* part of your life and relating to a lover is only *one* kind of relationship experience. *Life is full of other delights* and you have a responsibility to give all parts of your life the same value and attention. If you haven't been in a relationship for a while you may already have a very comfortable and full life. *You may even be scared of losing it.* Well you can't 'lose' it but you can end up giving it away when you start dating men. It is important that you make sure you keep the rest of your life when you get into a relationship.

♥ *You don't have to give up your life to be loved.*

Women are well known for obsessing about getting a relationship when they don't have one and for giving the rest of their lives up when they do. For millennia women have unfortunately been actively encouraged to focus all our energy on the man and his life, and it is a hard habit to beak. We have lived vicariously through men for long enough. One way you are guaranteed to throw your blasé attitude out of the window is to only care about getting a relationship and/or letting the rest of your life slip once you meet someone.

♥ *Your date(s) should fit into the life you already have.*

This means that:

- You are actively developing other areas of your life rather than waiting for a relationship to fill the void. Life is for living and you shouldn't waste a single day waiting for *anything*, let alone a relationship. A relationship may eventually come and take centre stage but your life has value and meaning even if it *never* does. Make sure you have plenty of other stuff going on *that you love*.
- You are not putting off any life decisions or changes until you meet someone. Buy the house, rent that flat, change career, go travelling, move to the country, lose the weight, go to college, write that book, have a child, go on holiday, start saving. *Do whatever it is you have been waiting to do if it is at all physically possible.* Start working towards it *today*.
- If a man asks you out when you are busy, you do not change your

plans to accommodate him. He has to wait if you are already doing something – end of story. If he doesn't ask again he isn't Mr W.

- You don't reserve times (like Saturday night) *just in case* he (or someone else) decides to ask you out or because you would rather go out with him than go to a film with a friend.
- Never blow out friends at the last minute for a date. Aside from being disrespectful to your friends, *you have a life that is worth preserving.* Your friendships are part of this and may well be there long after the date has gone by the way side.
- Keep your routine until the relationship develops and you are both ready to make small or gradual adjustments.
- You have a home; *keep living in it.* Don't spend all your time at your boyfriend's house until have agreed to get married (unless you have both explicitly agreed you are not *ever* going to marry, in which case, wait until you are living together.)

♥ *You have a life and it is worth something.*

3. Date lots of men

One of the principles of manifesting involves being *unattached to the outcome.* When it comes to women with low self-esteem and dating, being 'unattached' to the outcome can seem impossible. If you feel *'lucky to be asked'*, then you are unlikely to be 'unattached' to the outcome. Dating lots of men will help to give you the upper hand – not against men, but against your own insecurities about deserving to be asked out. The more men you get asked out by, the less attached you will be to what happens with each one. Yes, you may still prefer one particular guy over all the others but you know *there are plenty more* wherever he came from.

I have been dating on and off for four years and I can honestly say that I just don't take it anywhere near as seriously as I did when I first started. You simply become immune to it all. When you have been asked out on dozens of dates you don't get nervous, you don't start fantasising about being married to him (not with quite such fervour anyway!) and you just don't care so much if a guy doesn't call you or ask you out again, *because there are more in the pipeline waiting to meet you.* You stop getting hung up on 'him' and become much more able to take things in your stride. Suddenly there isn't anything to 'work out' or any reason to give him 'another chance' because you are emailing two other guys and meeting another next Friday! It really is his loss not yours.

It is *extremely challenging* to date only one guy in a blasé way. Make it easy on yourself; continue to date lots of men until you know you have met the right one *and* he has committed to you. (He can never be the right guy until he has committed.) However; *it is still better to date only one guy than to continue dating someone you know to be Mr Unavailable.*

4. Put up an ad or join an agency

Ok, so where are all these guys who are queuing to date you? Online, looking through personal ads, joined to a dating agency or a singles club, at speed dating or other singles events...

There are many benefits and downfalls to all the different ways you can meet men and dozens of books have been written on this subject. The more avenues you try the better because *you will be asked out by more men.* Remember, you are not doing this anxiously searching for Mr Wonderful – you are practising becoming blasé about going out with men *so you can be more choosey.* The more men who ask you out, the more opportunities for you to practice and the less likely you are to respond by feeling *lucky.*

♥ *Currently the single most effective way to get asked out by lots of men is to put up an ad.*

Believe me, if you do this you will soon become a dab hand at saying 'no thanks' and walking away. It is incredibly liberating when you finally realise that you *can* and that it really is no big deal. And every time you say 'no thanks' to Mr Not Right you climb another rung on the vibrational ladder, you confirm to the Universe that you are serious and not willing to settle for less than you want and deserve. You are moving on from your past way of doing things and the Universe *will* notice.

Dating can take over your life if you are not careful! While it may be tempting to treat each message you receive as a potential relationship, this will only lead to burnout and/or heartache. Your sole aim is to get dates. Until you are asked out, you are simply being 'browsed' so don't get too excited! Don't make the mistake of pouring your precious energy into long-winded email exchanges. Keep your messages short and sweet – if a guy wants to get to know you he will have to ask you out. And remember, until you have met him; *you do not know him so you can't possibly develop genuine feelings for him.*

The following dating tips will help you sort the wheat from the chaff quickly and effectively. They will also enable you to remain blasé and motivate the guys to ask you out. I highly recommend *The Rules for Online Dating* by Ellen Fein and Sherrie Schneider and *The Surrendered Single* by Laura Doyle, both of which are valuable dating resources. (Check the appendix for details.)

Some Savvy Dating Tips:

1. Never answer men's ads or send internet 'winks'. They come to you – full stop.

2. Don't respond to 'winks' or other similar prompts. Only respond to a proper email which has been clearly written for you.

3. Wait until the next day before replying to a message. And whatever you do, don't respond instantly to an email (or text) until you are properly established in a committed relationship.

4. If he hasn't asked you out by the fourth email stop responding. You are not looking for a pen pal and chatting won't motivate him. If he keeps emailing, don't send a response until he has categorically asked you out.

5. Never ask a man out, prompt him to contact you or make initial contact yourself.

6. Do not offer suggestions for when or where you meet. If he asks you to decide you can put it back to him by asking him what he suggests. If he is being vague, be vague back or simply don't reply until he asks you out properly.

7. Create a separate 'dating' email address. When he asks for your number/email give him this email address. You can use a pseudonym or online name if you want to protect your identity.

8. Don't give out your personal email address or your telephone number until you have met him at least three times. If you are using a dating website – use it for sending messages. If he says his subscription is running out and he wants to contact you, tell him you won't give out personal details until you have met someone. He will renew his subscription if he really wants to talk to you! If your subscription is running out, you can give him your dating email address if he asks.

9. If you meet a man in 'real life' circumstances, give him your dating email address rather than your number. Email gives you far more control over the dating process and is much safer until you know him. If you have to give him a number – make it a land line. Receiving texts from a man is potentially extremely invasive and far too easy for him. Texts can catch you off guard because he can text you day or night, wherever you are. Lazy men *love* sending texts; they are not so keen on actually picking the phone up and calling! Don't give him your mobile phone number until you have been on *at least* three dates or you already know the guy well. I gave my mobile number to a (polite) guy at work and he sent me inappropriate texts for weeks before I was able to get him to stop by threatening to go to the police. You don't need that hassle!

10. Do not get into instant messaging or texting back and forth until after the sixth date. Even then, keep it to a minimum.

11. He has to give you at least three days notice if he wants to see you – definitely no last minute dates, *especially* at the weekend.

12. He has to ask you out by Wednesday if he wants to see you Saturday night. You can count from when his email was sent or when he called rather than when you receive the message.

13. If he doesn't give you the details of the date (i.e. the time and/or place) when he asks you out *he needs to confirm with you at least 24 hours before you are due to meet.* Do not prompt him to give you the information. If you haven't heard from him 24 hours before the date *make other plans to go out and stick to them.* If he does get back to you within the 24 hours, you can either ignore him to see if he tries again, or you can say 'you didn't confirm the date so I made other plans'. Don't tell him about the deadline; *that is for your benefit.* If he is serious about seeing you, next time he will think twice about keeping you hanging on the end of a string.

14. It is not a date until he sets the date. If he has made vague arrangements to see you 'next weekend' or 'later in the week' carry on making plans. Never try to second guess when you will be seeing him or hold off other plans while he keeps you waiting. Better still, if he does get back to you with a more solid arrangement, be unavailable for the first day he suggests. He will continue to be vague about seeing you if you allow it by accommodating him. Men who make vague statements about when they will next see you are usually either not that bothered, playing games or simply expect you to fit in around their plans. None of these options are particularly attractive!

15. Never prompt a man in this dating process. If he can't figure it out, let him go around in his own little circles – don't get sucked into trying to straighten him out. It is more than likely that he just can't be bothered and you certainly won't motivate him by helping him out. If he does need a push, you are more likely to motivate him by *losing interest* in his fumblings than trying to get answers out of him. *He should be the one asking the questions.*

Let me tell you a little story about a guy I once started prompting:

I winked at a guy online and he responded. After four nice flowery emails from him, but no date, I decided that rather than ignore him, I would send him a cheeky email saying 'I joined match.com to meet men and to go on dates. I am not looking for a pen pal. All the best.'

He found this very amusing and surprised me by asking me out. I was about to go on holiday so we emailed a bit while I was away and when I returned we set about arranging the date. He expected me to decide where we were going and I told him that I'd prefer it if we go somewhere he suggested. We had our first date, which went well. I found him attractive and he was generous and interesting. He also seemed to like me and behaved like a gentleman.

After the first date I received a complimentary email from him. He had already told me he was going away for three weeks and so we continued an email conversation while he was away. During this time, he asked me if I wanted to book a plane ticket to go to Budapest with him. I felt flattered but was also concerned that he was asking me to do something risky when he had only met me once. When I said no, he seemed understanding about it, so I let it go.

Next, he suggested that I meet him at the airport at 11.45 pm. This certainly wasn't my idea of a second date! It was also incredibly presumptuous so I didn't reply to his email. Then, several days after he arrived, he emailed to let me know that he was back and to ask when I thought we should meet. By this time I had been waiting for four weeks for him to arrange the second date and he was still expecting me to organise it.

I was dying to prompt him, because we had got this far! It was really frustrating but when I realised I had been doing this from the beginning (winking, prompting him to ask me out and prompting him to decide where he was taking me on the first date), I realised that I would always be the one steering the relationship if I didn't make a stand and not prompt him again.

I replied something vague like 'it will have to be sometime next week.'

He replied 'Oh, that's a pity. I was hoping we could do something this weekend', but still didn't suggest when we could meet! By now I was feeling seriously annoyed as he had never even asked to see me at the weekend, so why was he mentioning it? I didn't reply. Several days later he sent me an email that literally read:

??
????????????????????????

This was a man who was going around in his own little circles and who had only suggested ridiculous things like going abroad together after only one date and me meeting him at the airport for our second date. I wished I had not wasted six weeks emailing him. I also realised that I should never have started prompting him, because once you start, the chances are you will have to continue doing all the work.

♥ ♥ ♥

Do yourself a favour; let *him* do the work. Let him find you. Let him ask you out. Let him decide when he wants to see you and where he is going to take you. *Don't be tempted to prompt him.* If he needs prompting then he really isn't your Mr Wonderful; he is simply wasting your time and engaging will only lower your vibration.

5. Keep your options open
Many dating books suggest keeping your options open because the guy may not be as keen on you as you are on him and it saves you getting hurt. While this is an extremely important reason for keeping your options open, it is not by any means the *only* one.

You need to go through the process of dating to find out if he is Mr Wonderful or Mr Unavailable. Before you get sexually or emotionally involved, you need to find out if *you* like *him* and if he is going to treat you properly. While you are taking this time to get to know someone, it is far easier to be blasé when you have more than one dating option open to you. And it is far easier to be choosey about whom you get involved with when you are blasé; if there is only one guy on your mind in the early stages, you will find it hard to remain detached and to observe his behaviour.

Many women feel that when a man asks them out they owe it to him to take themselves off the market until they see where it is going. *You owe a man absolutely nothing for asking you out.* Acting obliged reeks of low self-esteem and is the *opposite* of being blasé. This is not about playing hard to get, it is about *being hard to get*. If you are prone to 'desperate dating' (attaching too early) then keeping your options open really is the best antidote.

So, what does 'keeping your options' mean in real terms? It means not making a 'date' into a 'relationship' – *even in your head*. A date is a date. A relationship is something that develops over time and is based on mutual commitment. Just because a man has shown an interest in you and has asked you out it does not mean that you are embarking on a relationship with him. You are simply agreeing to meet with him so that you can get to know him a little better – *that is all*. While you are getting to know a guy:

- Meet/date as many men as you can
- Keep your ad(s) and/or profile up even when dating someone you really like
- Continue to pay any subscription fees for dating services
- Attend singles events
- Don't make 'future plans' with a date, i.e. holidays, weekends away, etc
- Don't spend too much time with a date (no more than twice in a week initially)
- Don't mentally decide 'he's the one' and screen out all other men literally or even in your head

6. Don't count your chickens

Men change their minds. He may start out really liking you and then suddenly go off the boil. *This is perfectly normal early on* which is why you 'date' him rather than getting instantly emotionally involved. Sometimes a man discovers that, although he finds you attractive, you just aren't the right woman for him. He is entitled to go through this process of discovery through dating, just as you are entitled to work out if he is the right man for you. It is really important not to take it personally if he changes his mind. It is not an indicator of your worth as a human being.

Make sure you don't ever count your chickens before they hatch – *even in your head*. A date is a date: nothing more nothing less. And if he doesn't call/email again; *he's just not interested enough*. You don't need to sweat it because you only want to be with a man who thinks you are the best thing since sliced bread!

7. Don't get sexually involved until he has successfully won you over

Learning to not 'give sex away' has been a huge lesson for me personally. Giving it away has caused me huge pain and heartache, not to mention eroded my self-esteem. I think that many, many women secretly believe that if they don't give sex fairly quickly the man will simply lose interest and go elsewhere. This has been one of the worst drawbacks to the so called 'sexual revolution'.

It seems that women are still allowing themselves to be sexually controlled. Today's women often feel that they are expected to be fully sexually available if they want to 'get' men rather than by being the chaste virgins of yesteryear. When I was a young adult I actually thought that having sex was how you initiated a relationship. If I liked someone, I had sex with them hoping they would still 'like' me and 'want' me the next morning. This is a *very* long way from sexual liber-ation. If you believe you have to give sex to get love, you are as much of a sexual slave as the woman who has to pretend to be a virgin to get a husband.

♥ *Sexual liberation is about having a choice over whether or not we have sex.*

25 reasons not to get sexually involved before he has success-fully won you over:

1. Women's bodies and sexuality belong to no one but themselves.
2. Your body belongs to no one but you.
3. Your sexuality is yours to share with whom you like, when *you* are good and ready.
4. Sex is sacred because it connects us to Source Energy.
5. Sex is sacred because it unites the Divine Masculine and Feminine Energies.
6. Sex is sacred because it creates new life.
7. Our bodies are sacred because they are the temples in which our spirit resides.
8. Your body is sacred because it is the Goddess incarnate.
9. If you 'give sex' to get a man's attention or to win his love then you are giving your body and your sacred sexuality away.
10. If you 'give sex' to a man to win his love, you are highly likely to fail and *you* will be the one left with the emotional fallout.
11. A man who shows an interest in you does not require you to have sex with him to show that you reciprocate.
12. A man who is *genuinely interested in you* will be happy to wait to have sex with you.
13. A man in love relishes the wait to sexually unite with his beloved.
14. A man who is willing to wait to have sex with you will experience *you as valuable* and *your relationship as special.*
15. A man who demands or expects sex as 'payment' for his attention or effort does not love *or* respect you.
16. When you give sex too early you seriously risk getting emotionally hurt.
17. When you give sex too early you won't know if a man is genuinely interested in you or if it is just convenient for him to be having sex with you.
18. When you give sex too early you won't know if he loves and respects you enough to wait for you.
19. When you give sex too early you deny yourself the opportunity to

be wooed.

20. When you give sex too early you are allowing yourself to get emotionally involved before you know if he is Mr Wonderful or Mr Unavailable.

21. When you give sex away to secure a relationship then you are devaluing yourself and therefore lowering your vibration.

22. Sex is not love: If you want or accept only sex, *then sex is all you will get.*

23. If you want to feel really special, valued and loved, then *give your man the pleasure of waiting for you.*

24. Not getting sexually involved with a date will help you remain blasé.

25. Not getting sexually involved too allows you to be *choosey.*

If you are considering having sex because you believe that is all you want from the encounter, make sure you are not kidding yourself. If you really like the guy, there is a strong chance that you are fooling yourself and falling into the trap of giving sex to try and secure love. Remember, once you have done it, you can't turn back the clock. And, if you are currently only looking for sex then you are vibrating on a sexual level. While there is nothing morally wrong with this, to manifest a loving relationship you need to be *vibrating from the heart, not the loins!*

♥ *You are only ready to manifest Mr Wonderful when you are ready to wait for love.*

When should you get sexually involved?

Well, it is always up to you when you have sex with a partner – there are no hard and fast rules. But if you are lacking in boundaries in this area, the following guidelines should help you. Remember, it is not about morals, it is about *emotional safety.* There is nothing morally wrong with having sex. However, it makes sense to only do it when you and the relationship are ready so that you avoid getting unnecessarily hurt and sending out the wrong message to the Universe. Waiting will ensure you know who you are getting involved with before you open yourself and your sacred body to them.

Don't even *consider* getting sexually involved until you have had at least *six proper dates* with a man (more on 'date six' below). If you have sexual boundary issues then six dates may seem like an impossible target. The more you practice, the easier it will become. If you blow it, don't be hard on yourself. It has taken me *years* to be able to risk not giving a man the sex I think he wants for fear that he will lose interest in me. Six dates really is the absolute earliest you should ever get sexually involved with a man if you want a special relationship with him. If he loses interest before date six, it is not because you haven't given him sex (unless he is Mr Sexual), it is because he is not the man for you and it is better to know this *before* you sleep with him.

This doesn't mean that you *should* have sex on date six; it means that you can *consider* it. I would, however, recommend that you don't have sex until you are in a committed relationship. It is not emotionally safe unless you have both agreed to commit to an exclusive relationship. Dating is not exclusive; you can both see other people. You hopefully will not be sleeping with anyone else, but by rights you can, and *so can he*. The commitment needs to be *explicit*. Being in a committed relationship should happen *because he has asked you*, not because one of you has made assumptions or you have asked him.

In *The Surrendered Single*,[2] Laura Doyle makes a really good suggestion which stops you having to ask him if he wants to be exclusive and it also gives you the chance to explain why you are not having sex with him. She suggests that when he tries to have sex with you, you simply tell him that you do not want to have sex outside of an exclusive relationship. This line is great because it puts the ball firmly in his court and at the same time you are taking responsibility for your sexual boundaries. This is not an attempt to control him – you're just stating the way it is for you.

However, *never say this to a man before date six*. You need at least six dates to get to know him and during the initial period you should be *observing* him. You don't owe him an explanation as to why you are not having sex with him. Just because he has asked you out doesn't mean he can expect sex from you. Only say it when *you are ready* for the relationship to progress. That should never be before date six because you simply haven't had enough time to discover who you are dealing with.

There is also the fact that if you mention 'exclusivity' to a man before the sixth date, you will come across as needy rather than choosey. If you have had six dates in quick succession (over three weeks or less) I would wait a bit longer, perhaps a month to six weeks. *Give yourself time.*

If a man wants to be 'exclusive' or is acting like he thinks you are before the sixth date, do not agree to it or go along with it because it is *too soon.* Just because he is enthusiastic doesn't mean he is 'the one'. You should be particularly cautious if he asks to make your relationship official within the first three dates. Don't be flattered, *be wary.* He may be Mr Passionate trying to knock you off your feet. Tell him it is too soon and you would like to spend more time getting to know him before you make a commitment. If he is genuine, he will be happy to wait until you are ready.

Once you feel sure that you are dealing with Mr Wonderful and that you trust the man you are dating, allow him to the opportunity to *ask you* to be exclusive. Only use 'the line' on him if he tries to come on to you and you feel the relationship is progressing the way that you want. Once you have said it, he should respect your wishes and not try to have sex until he has told you he wants to commit to you. If he says there and then that he wants to commit to you in response to your 'line', use your judgement to decide whether you think he is being honest or just trying to get sex. Chances are, if you have got past date six it is very unlikely that he is manipulating you. Men just don't work that hard unless they really want you. (And they know they don't need to as there are so many women out there willing to give them sex for absolutely nothing.)

You could also decide to wait until he has told you that he loves you. Again, be wary of men who gush within the first three dates, unless you have known well him for a while before you started dating. If he has told you that he loves you but hasn't brought up commitment (exclusivity) then use the line when he tries to initiate sex. If he tries to have sex with you before he has told you that he loves you – you may want to hold the line and wait until you also know that he loves you. This one is up to you. Some men are not forward in expressing their feelings, especially the British, so only wait if you think he is emotionally holding back or you want to be sure of his feelings before taking the plunge. Just make sure you never pre-empt him into telling you he loves you by telling him first or by saying you won't have sex until he has told you. That would really *not* be a good idea!

What is getting 'sexually involved'?

This is an important question because people have very varied ideas about what constitutes 'sex' or 'sexual involvement'. For the purposes of emotionally safe dating, 'sexual involvement' means *doing anything more than a kiss and a cuddle*. It includes sleeping in the same bed and 'doing nothing' and it includes rolling around in a passionate frenzy, with all your clothes on. 'Sexual involvement' certainly includes doing *anything* that involves sexual organs. Kissing is good because it helps you to bond and discover if there is any chemistry. It will also keep his interest and the romance going while you get to know each other.

Rather than trying to work out what you are 'allowed to do', take responsibility for deciding where your personal boundaries lie. The closer and more intimate you get physically, the more sexually charged and emotionally vulnerable you become. Once the sexual energy takes over, it will make it hard for you to see him clearly and you will feel more attached to him, making you less able to be blasé and choosey. Do what makes sense – keep *all* of your sexual boundaries in place until you know it is completely safe to bring them down.

♥ *Sexual boundaries should be the final frontier.*

Keeping your sexual boundaries while dating

There are other emotional boundaries which protect us from someone getting close enough to invade our sexual boundaries. In the early days of dating there are some things to avoid doing:

- Never assume that because he is a friend or someone you have known for a long time that you already know him *well enough* to bypass having any boundaries.
- Always trust your instincts – if it doesn't feel right don't do it.
- A friend can recommend a guy, but unless she has been also out with him, she doesn't *really* know what he will be like.
- Avoid alcohol and drugs when in the early stages of dating. If you must drink, keep it to an absolute minimum.
- Don't give out your mobile number until you are ready for the relationship to develop. Texting makes us think that we know someone better than we do and can easily take us off guard. If he already has your number, keep texting to a minimum, avoid sexual texts and wait at least an hour before responding while in the early stages. This gives you a chance to compose yourself before responding.
- Don't let a guy into your house during dates 1-3. Even if you already know him, don't invite him in after a date for at least dates 1-3. *You are in new territory when you are dating and need to set new boundaries.* There is no need to rush the process just because he is not a complete stranger. If it seems weird because he has been in your house before, just say you are tired and going to bed. This way you will be much less likely to end up in bed with him!
- Don't hang out at each other's houses until you have had six official dates. You can spend time at each other's houses when he has asked you to be his girlfriend.
- Don't spend too much time together or do anything that involves 'sleeping over' until you are ready to get sexually involved. Keep your distance so you don't get sucked into doing something sexual before you are ready.

8. Don't consider him serious until he has asked you out at least six times

Most blind (internet) dates don't get past the first meeting because you just can't tell what the chemistry is going to be until you meet them. However, just because a guy asks you out two or three times it doesn't mean that it is serious; it means that you both liked each other enough to meet again and *that is all*.

If a man can't keep his attention and effort going for six dates then he's *'just not that into you'*. And if a man is going to give up, he will do so before date six. A man simply won't make that much effort for a woman he is not that serious about. And if a woman likes a guy, she needs to allow at least six dates to find out if he is serious about her before she even considers that things are potentially 'going somewhere'.

It takes a lot of effort for a man to date a woman six times, especially if there is no sex involved. And by 'date' I don't mean 'see', I mean actually ask her out, organise where you are going, pay for you, and take you somewhere nice – even if it is for a walk or a coffee. It *doesn't* take a man much effort to invite you to join him and his mates and to take you home for sex at the end of the night. That takes no effort at all and is certainly not a 'date'; it is just convenient sex.

If a man is serious about you he will *enjoy* taking you out and making the effort to impress you. So, don't consider him serious about you until he has *taken you out* on at least six dates.

9. Don't consider it a relationship until it is exclusive

Women like to know things are 'official' because they know instinctively that it isn't a relationship until the guy makes a request for exclusivity. You shouldn't be trying to guess where you stand or making assumptions. Do your self a favour, be blasé and keep dating other men until he has made a pledge for your heart. Even if he wants to spend all his time with you and you doubt he is seeing anyone else – or even if he has told you he isn't – *he still needs to ask you to be exclusive with him*. Asking you out is the first step. Asking for your commitment is the next. It isn't a 'relationship' until it is exclusive.

10. Create some real hurdles

While you are dating men, you need to create some hurdles. It is not about making it hard for him in order to be 'gamey'; it is so you can get to know if he is both serious about you *and* considerate towards you. I have discovered that men who want to see you will be willing to work for the privilege. If a man won't jump a hurdle, he is either not that into you or he is Mr Unavailable.

A game player will reveal himself very quickly when you expect something of him and you will soon find out what he is really like. If a man is only willing to do things on his terms you need to know about it sooner rather than later. You can find that out by creating the following six hurdles:

First hurdle: *He has to be the one to ask you out.* Never chase a man, even if the carrot is the biggest, juiciest, sexiest carrot you have ever seen. Always ignore a dangling carrot and move on.

Second hurdle: *He has to organise the date properly.* He does this by giving you plenty of notice (three days), telling you in advance a time/place to meet and by suggesting a place to go. If he asks you to decide where to go, ask him what he suggests. Never go out on a date without proper notice.

Third hurdle: *He has to be on time.* If he is late he should at least explain why and apologise. (He is only *really* sorry if he doesn't do it again next time.) Most men are on time for the first date but not necessarily after that. He has to be *consistently* on time. If he keeps you waiting more than five minutes he is being rude and not valuing your time. After he has been late once, if he is more than ten minutes late again, don't see him. End the date by going home or not answering your door. You can give him one more chance after ending the date if you think he has got the message. Otherwise, don't see him again, especially if you know he was more than twenty minutes late. I had one guy who turned up twenty minutes late on the second date and fifty minutes late for the third! If you accept lateness, then that's what you will get.

Forth hurdle: *He has to offer to pay for you on the date.* A man who doesn't offer or obviously resents paying because he makes comments about it is not a gentleman. He has forgotten what it means to take a woman out and make her feel special and cared for. If he is like this when he is trying to impress you, imagine what he will be like once he thinks he has got you! Spare yourself the heartache – ditch him. You don't even need to stay for the duration of the date. If he doesn't offer to pay, don't allow yourself to be prompted into paying. Sometimes simply sitting down will let him know what you expect. If he doesn't get the hint, make your excuses and leave.

Fifth hurdle: *He has to pick you up and take you home when he takes you out.* I put this after paying for the date because if you meet a man through internet dating or you don't know him well it is best that you don't give him your address before you have met him at least once. If he already knows where you live or you have met him before then you would expect him to pick you up on the first date.

If he doesn't offer to collect you then you *can* prompt him about this as many men think women don't want to be escorted or give out their address. When he suggests meeting somewhere just say something like 'I'd prefer it if you pick me up' or 'I'd prefer you meet me at my house so we can go together'. Picking you up doesn't necessarily mean driving you somewhere – it may mean walking or getting a cab with you. If he objects or argues just say 'we can go another time when it is convenient for you to pick me up'. (This also something Laura Doyle suggests in *The Surrendered Single*[3] and it has worked for me.)

I have only had a negative reaction from a guy once and he was *most* indignant with me. He was seriously aggressive and rude about it. He only lived a ten minute walk from my house and he wasn't prepared to go out of his way because we were heading in the opposite direction. Thankfully, I managed not to engage in an argument with him and I was really, really glad to find out that he was so aggressive and unwilling before getting involved with him.

If you have met a guy once and you still don't feel safe enough with him to give him your address – ask yourself if you should be having a second date at all. If you want to be cautious – you can always get him to pick you up somewhere near you home. It is important that you know he cares enough to escort you to and from your home.

Sixth hurdle: *He has to ask you if you will commit to being in a relationship with him.* Until that happens, continue being blasé!

If a man is serious about you these 'hurdles' will be a cinch for him. He will fly over them because his masculine passion has been ignited and he naturally flows toward you, allowing nothing to get in his way. If he stumbles at any of the above how can you possibly imagine a long term relationship with him? Imagine getting married or having children with him if he won't pay for your coffee! If he can't manage the above he's either not that into you or he has no intention of treating you the way you deserve to be treated. These hurdles are reasonable challenges that enable him to prove he is worthy of your love and commitment.

Sticking to these hurdles can be extremely challenging when you feel lucky to have a guy's attention. You can worry that it will put him off when you think that you should be encouraging him. If he is right for you, he won't need you to encourage him; *his masculine energy will be driven to get to you.* Having these hurdles in place will not only emotionally protect you and give you standards to check his behaviour against; they will also show him you are valuable and *choosey.*

Remaining Unattached to the Outcome

I had a client who told me of her experience of manifesting relationships. The woman had set out to manifest a relationship and when an attractive guy came along she felt she had got exactly what she asked for. She described to me all the amazing details and fated coincidences involved in meeting her boyfriend. She was clearly wowed by the power of manifesting.

Because he seemed to fit the bill (ticked all the boxes) and it felt 'fated' and she proceeded with the relationship thinking she had successfully manifested Mr Wonderful. Well, she *had* successfully manifested a relationship and she enjoyed experiencing all the powerful fated feelings associated with the arrival of a manifestation. However, what she wasn't aware of was that she had manifested from a certain emotional level and had attracted a partner from that vibration. The ticked boxes and the fated feeling were all it took for her to decide to attach to him *and the outcome.*

Unfortunately, the emotional vibration of the man she manifested wasn't actually what she *really* wanted and she didn't find this out until she was already emotionally and sexually involved. Though they hadn't jumped straight into bed, they did jump straight into the relationship. By the time she came to see me her relationship had already ended after an intense whirlwind romance.

Neither partner was detached from the outcome because both were 'star struck' by the power of manifesting. They didn't think they had anything to worry about because their manifesting had 'worked'; they had found a tick box lover! What they didn't realise was that *just because something has been consciously manifested doesn't mean it is what you really want.*

When you manifest a relationship you cannot afford to rush to conclusions. Manifesting Mr Wonderful is not the same as manifesting a car parking space. You have to find out what is inside the gift of a relationship before you will know if it is right for you. Just as you take a car for a test drive before you buy it or look around a house before you rent it, you need the chance to decide if a relationship fits *before* you emotionally invest.

- We manifest from the level of our recent emotional vibration, *especially* in relationships.
- It is our job to raise our vibration if we want to manifest at a higher level.
- It is our job to remain unattached to the outcome of how and when we will reach our goal.
- It is our job to keep our eyes open and to observe before we whole-

heartedly accept what we have manifested. (This makes us less likely to get caught up in a low vibration relationship.)

- You *always* need to check a suitor out before getting involved just as you would try on a pair of shoes before you buy them.

It is relatively easy to manifest a relationship; the real challenge lies in manifesting one higher up the vibrational relationship ladder. You can only do this by raising your vibration and by *making sure you check out the emotional level of the relationship before you say 'yes please' to the Universe's delivery.* And you can only hope to do this if you remain *unattached to the outcome.* If you are working at raising your vibration there will almost certainly be a time delay before you start receiving offers from men with a higher vibration. You have to work your way up the vibrational ladder and be patient with the process.

♥ *When you manifest a new love interest it is essential to remain detached from the outcome with him.*

The Art of Manifesting

Once you are able to work with the 12 Principles of the Law of Attraction, you are ready to ask the Universe for what you really want. So far you have been clearing, designing and ploughing, ready to plant seeds. You know the difference between Mr Wonderful and Mr Unavailable: that he treats you well and makes you feel good. But what makes him *your* Mr Wonderful? And how do you send out a signal to the Universe that you are ready for him?

Raising your vibration will naturally change the kind of men you attract over a period of time. If you are practising being blasé and choosey, you will be sending the Universe a strong message about what you want. There is, however, no harm in practising a little manifesting 'magic' while you are getting on with your savvy dating. This is the 'fun' side of manifesting!

There are several ways we can ask the Universe to deliver what we want. Below are some useful manifesting techniques you can try.

However, it is important to only do them when you are ready to start manifesting a relationship with Mr Wonderful because you feel capable of saying 'no' to Mr Unavailable. These techniques will help to crystallise your desires and send your wishes out to Source, but they are *not* a replacement for raising your emotional vibration.

When you use these techniques *you will manifest* but your manifestations will always reflect your emotional vibration. Don't expect the first man to come along to be your Mr Wonderful. *Give yourself at least six dates to check suitors out.* Remember, any inappropriate men you attract will give you a valuable opportunity to say 'no thanks' and to help you clarify both what you want and what you believe you deserve. Good luck!

1. The Dream Scenario
2. The Wish List
3. Affirmations
4. Become the Flower
5. Invite Him In

Though you can dip into these activities as you wish, they have been designed to be done in the order they have been written because they are interlinked. The first activity will really get things going and is good to do even if you don't want to try anything else. It provides a good foundation for the other manifesting techniques as it will help you clarify what you want.

1. The Dream Scenario

Imagine you have a magic wand and you can create the man and the relationship you want *exactly as you want it*. During this exercise you are coming from a place of strong self-esteem and high expectations of what you deserve. It is *completely up to you* what happens; you are in control of your Dream Scenario.

You can do this exercise with a friend or by yourself. If you have a friend helping you, get her to read the instructions and to make notes of what you say. If you are alone you can tape the instructions and listen to it or read it through a few times before you start.

Activity 4
Find a time when you can be quiet and won't be disturbed.
Have some A4 paper (or a journal) and a pen ready.

a. **Close your eyes and take a few deep breaths – connect to your core and to the Source.** Allow yourself to feel those blissful feelings. Ask your Higher Self to guide you through this exercise.

b. **Now, still with your eyes closed, imagine meeting Mr Wonderful.** Picture the scene – where are you and what are you doing? Imagine him coming up to you and showing that he is interested. What does he look like? What is he wearing? How does he approach you? What kind of a person is he? What does he do? First imagine it – looking for as many details as possible – then record it or get your friend to write it for you while you talk with your eyes still closed.

c. **Next, close your eyes and imagine he has asked you out.** Imagine the date – where does he take you? What are you both wearing? Imagine the date and remember you have the magic wand so you can let your imagination run wild with you. Picture the date with all the details. When he has brought you home you can open your eyes and write about the dream date in as much detail as possible.

d. **Skip forward and imagine you are in a committed relationship with him.** Picture yourself married or living with him – whichever you eventually want. Imagine your home and lifestyle together. How do you share a life together? What kind of things do you do together? Imagine waking up with him on a Saturday and spending the day with him. Now write about your life with Mr Wonderful with as much detail as possible. Don't censor it; it is your imagination, your dream. Don't question what is possible – imagine what you would have with Mr Wonderful if anything *was* possible.

If you imagine someone you know while you do this exercise it doesn't automatically mean he is your Mr Wonderful – it means he has some of the qualities of your Mr Wonderful which you need to consider. Many men will have important aspects of what you are looking for even if they are not ultimately right for you. Use this exercise to help you visualise *what is possible*. You are not attaching to a particular outcome with a specific person – you simply allowing yourself to imagine your dream scenario so you can identify the qualities you are looking for. Being specific about details helps you to do this.

2. The Wish List

You can use your 'dream scenario' to help you compile a wish list or you can do it off the top of your head. Again you can do this alone or with a friend.

Activity 5

First write an uncensored wish list (preferably after doing the dream scenario so Mr W and your relationship with him is fresh in your mind). Put everything you want about him and the relationship on your list. Again, don't be realistic – imagine you are giving the list to your very own fairy Godmother! Write down physical attributes and character. Write what he does and what he likes doing with you. List *everything* you want in a man/relationship.

Once you have a complete uncensored list, create space for four separate lists:

1. Absolutely essential
2. Would be great
3. Not too bothered
4. Could tolerate

Read through your wish list and sort each item, adding them to one of the first three categories, being as honest as you can. Nothing on your initial list will go onto the 'could tolerate' list but some things may need clarifying when you come to categorise them and this extra category may come in useful.

Example 1: You may discover under scrutiny that it isn't 'essential' that he is over 6 foot but it *is* essential, for you, that he is taller than you. Put 'over six foot tall' on the 'would be great' list and 'taller than me' on the 'absolutely essential' list.

Example 2: You may originally have put 'non- smoker' on your list, but would you tolerate someone who had the odd cigarette on a night out? If so, put non-smoker under 'would be great' and social smoker under 'could tolerate'.

Example 3: 'He rides a bicycle'. Be specific, does he ride a bike to work? Use a bike instead of a car? Has fun biking at the weekend? Or enjoys long cycling trips?

Be as specific as you can and really think about what it is that you want and how important it is. Essential items should only cover things you would *have to have* to consider being with a guy. Also, make sure it is all in the positive; that you are listing what you *do* want rather than what you *don't* want. It is important that you get the wording right.

Examples:

'Not addicted' should read something like 'emotionally balanced' and/or 'has a healthy lifestyle'

'Not obsessed with his previous girlfriend/wife' should read 'emotionally available'

'Doesn't smoke' should read 'non-smoker'

Once you have sorted the wish list into the three or four categories, you can review it periodically. The list should never be set in stone – it is a guideline, something to aim for which will probably change over time. However, you do need to know what your bottom line is with regards to getting involved with a man.

The Bottom Line

♥ *The bottom line is that he is fully emotional available to be with you today, that he asks you out and that he treats you well.*

He may tick everything else on your wish list but if he doesn't meet the

bottom line criteria, *he is not your Mr Wonderful*. You can add an item
or two to your bottom line. If you know you desperately want children
and he *has* to be open to having children for you to consider getting
involved, then add 'wants children' to your bottom line. However, *use
the bottom line very sparingly*. Most things will go on the essentials
list. Ask yourself, if you met a man who you fell deeply in love with
and he didn't want children, is there any chance you would change your
mind? If there is any chance you could do without something, don't
make it your bottom line; put it on the essentials list instead.

♥ *Remain unattached to the outcome with a date until you know he
meets your bottom line criteria.*

You won't necessarily know or have to find out if he meets the bottom
line criteria immediately. *This is why you have hurdles and a six date
rule.* These boundaries will help you decide if he does meet your
bottom line criteria before you get emotionally involved. You will
usually know much sooner than date six, often by the end of the first or
second date. But if you don't know very early don't jump the
relationship gun – give yourself the six dates to check him out and
complete the full hurdle challenge.

What if he doesn't tick the boxes?

You may come across a man who meets your bottom line criteria who
you also find attractive but who doesn't score well on you wish list.
Don't rule him out just because he doesn't tick the boxes. Being
unattached to the outcome includes being open to what sort of package
you receive from the Universe. Life can surprise us. Sometimes we
need something from a person that we are not conscious of and the
Universe will send this to you when you are ready.

It is important not to get too caught up in the tick boxes. They help
you focus and send your desires out to Source but they are not a hard
and fast rule. You may say it is essential that he is taller than you then
meet a man who is the same height or shorter and fall madly in love

with him. I generally like my men over six foot and one of my big loves was an inch shorter than me which actually turned out to be surprisingly nice. Unfortunately he was also a long shot from the bottom line criteria, but falling for him did make me realise that I could actually fall in love with someone and feel comfortable with them being shorter than me! At the end of the day what really matters is your bottom line – and that is *always non-negotiable*.

♥ *Love is mysterious but a bottom line is still a bottom line.*

Future plans on your wish list

Wanting a man who will marry you, give you children, or move to India with you fall under the heading of 'future plans'. It is particularly important that you don't start questioning a man about these things in the first few dates. He may reveal his wishes on his internet profile, in his ad or when he meets you the first or second time. He may even ask you directly what you want. But if he doesn't bring it up, don't ask. If he feels strongly one way or the other, he will usually let you know pretty quickly. If he doesn't let you know that he isn't the marrying kind, or that he loves children and dreams of a large family, take it that he is currently neutral.

All you need to know at the beginning is if he is fully emotionally available to be with you, able to treat you well and whether or not you are compatible. Once he starts to fall in love with the right woman, a man will often start to want things that he didn't know he wanted. If he is not in love or you are not with the right woman for him, he will often withhold what he knows he ultimately wants.

Having said this, if a man is adamant about something right from the start, *listen to him*. Don't fool yourself into thinking you can make him change his mind one way or the other. If you get involved with him when you know from the beginning that you don't want the same things, you are taking a big risk. If he hasn't changed his mind six months down the line – it is wise to assume he is not going to and to get out of the relationship. If you want to take the 'six month risk' minimise your involvement with him so if you decide to get out, you don't feel like you have lost a leg.

Using your wish list

Creating a wish list should be a fun activity where you clarify what you dream of in a relationship with a man. (You can also use wish lists for other areas of your life.)

- While the list should be positive and clear, be flexible to allow for surprises.
- It is not a replacement for the bottom line criteria; treat it as the cherry on the cake.
- Don't use the wish list to judge the men you meet, or to jump to conclusions about your manifestations – use it to fire your manifesting powers of imagination and enthusiasm.
- Once you have created the wish list, you can use it for the other exercises.

When you have a comprehensive wish list that you have spent time clarifying and tweaking in your journal, you can write a special version of it to 'send' to the Universe.

It is suggested that you also read the section on affirmations before doing the following activity.

Activity 6

You can do this task by yourself or with like-minded friends. Get a nice piece of paper, an envelope and a pretty pen. You can also use decorations or coloured sparkly pens.

Take your finished wish list and write a simple version of it. Only include the 10-15 most important things and make sure your bottom line is in there, but you don't need to call it your bottom line – just put it at the top of the list. You can write it as a letter:

Dear Universe,

I really want a relationship with Mr Wonderful where I feel...

With a man who....

Or you can write it as a list;

I attract Mr Wonderful into my life. He is...

It is worth writing a few rough drafts to get it just right. These are just examples. If you want more help with the wording check the section on affirmations. Imagine you are like a child writing to Father Christmas – it needs to be fun and just right for you!

Once you have completed the special wish list, connect to Source. While you are connected, read the letter/list out-loud to the Universe. If you are with friends you can make it into a ceremony and read the lists in front of each other. Then fold your wish list up and put it in the envelope. You can either seal it or tuck the flap in, but you now leave the rest to the Universe. Put the envelope somewhere safe until you want to review your list or you have found your man.

3. Affirmations

You have already used affirmations to help you develop self-esteem. 'I am lovable', 'I am loved', 'I am love' are all self-esteem building affirmations. Using affirmations is a powerful way to change the way you think and feel. Learning how to use them effectively will be invaluable to you in both raising your vibration and for attracting what you want into your life. When you use affirmations you are breaking internal thought/feeling patterns and telling the Universe what you expect to experience.

What is an affirmation?

An affirmation is a short phrase which 'affirms' something for you.

♥ *Affirmations affect your subconscious thoughts and feelings and will also act like a 'prayer' because the message is an energy vibration that reverberates into the Universe.*

We are constantly giving ourselves 'messages' about our beliefs. These internal messages have a *huge* energetic impact, especially if there are strong feelings attached to them. If we give ourselves negative messages, whether said out-loud or in our head, we vibrate negatively. Therefore, how we 'self talk' has a profound impact on the quality of our life and our experiences. If we are prone to negative 'self talk' we can gradually change by using positive affirmations. It is because affirmations are so effective at raising your vibration (by changing the way you think and feel) that they form an integral part of the practice.

You can also use affirmations to attract what you want into your life. *What you say will come true if you feel it strongly enough.* Our self-talk has a strong energetic vibration because we are co-creators, so our messages will be energetically attracting things to us, for good or ill. Remember – *everything is energy*; like attracts like; thoughts and emotions are powerful energy vibrations. So if we say what we want and keep affirming it with strong emotions then what we want will naturally be attracted to us. You can literally will something into being by thinking about it because your thoughts and the feelings attached to them are energy vibrations which attract manifestations.

♥ *When you use affirmations you are telling the Universe what you expect and so it will be manifested.*

Creating effective affirmations
Affirmations are relatively easy to create but there is an art to making them effective. When you use an affirmation you are saying 'yes please' to the Universe, therefore it is important to make sure that you are saying 'yes please' to what you really want. The most effective affirmations are positive, clear, have a strong emotional resonance with you and are worded in the present tense:

- To attract positively, we must send out positive energy so it is vital that you are asking for what you *do* want rather than what you *don't* want and that you ask it *in a positive manner*. Affirmations should be *stated in the positive*; 'I want a loving man' instead of 'I want a man who isn't a womaniser or a cheat'. Also, make sure there aren't any subtle negative feelings hidden in what you say; 'I want a man who will get around to asking me out' should read something like 'I am ready to be asked out'. The first affirmation sounds like you don't expect to be asked out, the second sounds like you believe *being asked out is a given*, now that you are ready.

• An affirmation needs to be clear and simple so that the Universe knows exactly what you are asking for. Try and keep it short and precise: 'I am ready for love' or 'I invite Mr Wonderful into my life' rather than 'I have an open heart so I can attract and receive a loving, caring, sexy man who wants to spend the rest of his life with me and give me children'. In trying to keep it precise I came up with the name 'Mr Wonderful' because to me the term means a man who can fulfil my desires. It is a term which encapsulates what I want. You can come up with a different name or way to convey what you want but *keep it simple* rather than writing a long wordy affirmation.

• If an affirmation has little emotional resonance for you then it will not be as powerful because *your feelings have the biggest impact on the energy vibrations you send out*. This means if you use other people's affirmations – make sure they really speak to *you*. You can make adjustments to someone else's affirmations if you would prefer not to start from scratch. I would suggest, however, that you try to come up with something for yourself. An affirmation you have come up with is more likely to have emotional resonance and the process of finding a good affirmation will further help you clarify what you want. Also, when you come up with a good one it is exciting, which will add emotional potency to your affirmation.

• Affirmations need to be worded in the present. Ultimately tomorrow never comes, so stating affirmations in the future tense instantly puts them out of reach. State your affirmation as if it is *already true* by wording it in the present tense. The Universe will then work to bring it to you *today*. The more you 'act as if' you already have what you want, that you are where you want to be, the more powerful your manifesting energy will be. You are not requesting it, you are stating that 'it is already so'. Not only does this demonstrate incredible faith and self belief (which creates a positivity that is hard to beat) but the Universe has to bring into being *what is*: By stating 'what is' before it exists, you create a vacuum which the Universe must fill.

• Although you can word your affirmations as desires or wants, I believe that it is more powerful to show that you *expect to receive* something rather than you are *hoping it will arrive*. The words 'I want' have negative connotations for many of us which can get in the way of manifesting. Many people, especially in Britain, grew up hearing things like 'I want doesn't get' and were told not to say 'I want' when they asked for something. Apparently stating what you want is seen as selfish and/or rude. Perhaps more importantly, in terms of affirmations, 'wanting' is what we do *when we haven't yet got something*. For some of us it can have a connotation of feeling 'desperate'. For the purpose of affirmations we want to create the 'already got it' vacuum to encourage the Universe to deliver. 'I attract...' or 'I am ready...' or 'I receive...' or 'I invite...' or even, if you are feeling really daring 'I have...' or 'I enjoy...' (because I already have) are further down the process from wanting and closer to the experiencing. However, if you usually feel guilty for 'wanting' it can also be really affirming to unashamedly *state your wants* to the world! (Use 'I want' or 'I desire' for your wish list.) Be proud of your desires – without them you couldn't be a co-creator.

To create an affirmation, try to summarise what it is you want. You can go back to your wish list or dream scenario and try to make the picture into a concise statement – almost like a mission statement that will help to focus yourself and the Universe. Play with ideas and allow yourself to be creative.

If you feel you have to go through a few phases to become ready to get what you ultimately want then begin with affirmations that reflect where you need to get to first. For example, if you feel you need to work on being able to receive positive attention from men then start with that; 'I am open to positive male attention' or 'I enjoy receiving positive male attention'. It is not useful to go for your ultimate goal until you feel ready in yourself because it will be harder to believe in what you are saying and therefore more challenging to feel positive. Build your relationship confidence gradually starting with the first step not the final destination.

Using affirmations

Once you have had a go at developing some affirmations you need to actually *use* them. While it is valuable to go through the process of creating affirmations – if you don't get around to using them, they won't work. An affirmation is different from a wish list. When you create a wish list you say it to the Universe and then *let it go*. Affirmations, on the other hand, have to be repeated because they are used for aligning your internal vibration with what you are trying to create. You have to 'work them' so that they sink into your deeper self and have the chance to transform your emotional energetic vibration.

♥ *Affirmations are about changing how you feel inside and aligning your energy with what you want to manifest.*

If you know on a deep level that you deserve love and state that you are already enjoying a loving relationship, then the Universe has no choice but to deliver it to you in order to fill the vacuum. To make this shift you have to repeat affirmations regularly. You are self-talking all day long so you need to get a conscious word in edgeways. If you don't say it regularly then your message will simply get lost in all the other inner babble.

♥ *The key to using affirmations is to repeat them regularly.*

- Whenever you say an affirmation, repeat it several times
- Say it out-loud and/or in front of a mirror for added potency
- Write your affirmations down

- Post them around your home as reminders
- Only work with one (or two) affirmations at a time
- Work with each affirmation for *at least* one week
- Repeat your affirmation several times during the day
- Having a routine can help you remember to say your affirmations
- You can use an alarm to remind you the next time to repeat them
- Say it whenever you remember during the day – even if you only have time to say it once or twice
- *For maximum benefit first connect with Source, then say your affirmation from this powerful feeling state*

If you find it hard to feel anything about an affirmation it is worth playing around with it until it sounds just right to you. Sometimes when we have a wall of negativity or doubt standing between us and what we want it can be hard to get excited about an affirmation. If you find yourself in this situation, don't worry – *just 'act as if' you believe in it* for the time being. This will give you a chance to get started and the messages will get through – though they may take a little longer. Here are some affirmations you can use and/or adapt:

- ♥ *'I enjoy a loving relationship with Mr Wonderful'*
- ♥ *'I attract a wonderful man into my life'*
- ♥ *'I am open to receiving love'*
- ♥ *'I am a beacon of light guiding my beloved home'*
- ♥ *'I invite Mr Wonderful to ask me out'*
- ♥ *'I experience the joy of being truly loved'*
- ♥ *'I experience the bliss of being united with my soulmate'*

While you are travelling on this journey if you stumble across an inner block or negative belief that is hard to shift, use affirmations. You can add new ones to your (daily) practice that are pertinent to you. Affirmations work when you work them.

4. Become the Flower

If you have difficulty receiving from a man this one is definitely for you. We have explored the differences between men and women and the nature of sexual attraction. I have suggested that we women should behave like the 'choosey egg' and create hurdles. You could also say that women are like flowers and men are like bees – creatures that just can't resist the scent and colour of a beautiful flower. Bees seek flowers in the way that men seek women, and out of this intense attraction, together they create both honey *and* new life. What an inspiration!

Many women have forgotten their innate 'flower' nature and some complain that 'flowers' are passive and judged solely by appearance. I, however, believe we have a lot to learn from the medicine of the ultra feminine 'flower energy' – a woman who embraces her essential flower nature is a sight to behold for both sexes.

In her radiance she will attract many 'bees' who seek out her nectar. She can bask in their busy attention and desire to get close to her. A flower is not passive because she is *actively attracting* the bee's energy, by connecting with her glorious self. While the flower and the bee do have opposite roles to play, the relationship is symbiotic and therefore *equal*. The special relationship between flowers and bees (or other nectar sucking insects) symbolise the cosmic sexual dance between the masculine and feminine.

♥ *If you want to attract more positive male attention you must become 'the flower'.*

Make sure you are ready to deal with male attention and that you are reasonably equipped to both recognise and deal with Mr Unavailable before trying this, as you may well receive some unwanted attention in the flurry! It is important that once you get some male attention that you remember you are the choosey egg and make sure you don't let every 'busy bee' into your personal space.

Becoming the flower is a state of mind. If you have difficulty with seeing yourself as an attractive, beautiful flower that men are going to want to get close to, then you can start with affirmations, something like: 'I am a beautiful flower' or 'I embrace my inner flower' or 'I become the flower'. You can change the word from flower to feminine or Goddess if it feels better for you.

All women are flowers inside, even if they have forgotten what it feels like. And men are nowhere near as picky about what women look like as women believe. Men respond to women who *feel and behave like flowers* even if they are not some amazing, exotic orchid. Men instinctively know when a woman is in her feminine energy, *even if she is not his type* – and they respond positively even if they don't want to 'follow up' with a date or a relationship.

♥ *All you need to do is make contact with your inner flower and allow her to unfurl.*

Thinking like the flower will raise your sexual energy vibration. You will be sending out strong sexual signals to the bees, which is why it is important to be ready before you do it! Becoming the flower makes you feel attractive and feminine which will automatically make you more attractive to the opposite sex. *Bees are always on the look out for flowers to admire.* It is important to remember that you are not seeking your worth through male attention because y*ou already know you are intrinsically valuable.* When you become the flower, you are embracing your Divine Feminine Energy which will naturally give off an attractive signal to the opposite sex. In fact, you will also find that women will give you compliments.

Next you need to *act* like a flower. A flower presents herself to the world with pride in her innate beauty. A woman who puts her belief that she is beautiful into action automatically becomes more beautiful because *she is shifting her sexual energy vibration up a gear.* This is really not about becoming what you think men want you to be, *it is about becoming who you truly are; a beautiful sexual Divine Being.*

Men enjoy you being who you truly are because they were born to desire you. You can't blame them for that! No one is saying that you are *only* a flower; there are of course many other valuable aspects to you as well. However, if you want to step into the mating game, or if you just want to embrace your Divine Femininity and your miraculous female body, then acting like you are a flower is just the ticket – and it is really fun *when you do it for your self.*

Acting like a flower means adorning and making the most of your Divine Femininity which resides in your body. Following are some suggestions for bringing your inner flower out into the light of day. Even if you already embrace your femininity, there is no harm in doing a little more or in trying something you haven't done before, or don't do very often. Try wearing more of the following:

- Feminine clothes, especially skirts
- Floral patterns or flower jewellery
- A flower (or butterfly) clip in your hair
- Pretty jewellery, accessories and/or hats
- Nice shoes, especially with a heel (it doesn't have to be high)
- Something which is a pretty or bright colour – even if it is just a scarf or a bracelet
- Clothes that flatter your shape
- A bit of make up and/or lip gloss
- Beautiful or sexy underwear

You could also try any or all of the following;

- Paint your nails
- Grow your nails and/or your hair long(er)
- Wear your hair down or in a new style
- Get your hair coloured or treated
- Go for a pampering – a massage, facial or manicure
- Indulge in sensual bath oils or body products… umm!
- Try a new perfume or body spray
- Consult an expert on your wardrobe, makeup or hair
- Show a little more of your cleavage, legs or accentuate your waist –

which ever you think is your greatest asset

Make an effort to display your inner flower whenever you go out, even if it is just popping down the road. All you have to do is pop a flower clip in your hair, or put on a pretty bracelet and some lip gloss, or put a nice pair of shoes to remind yourself that you are indeed a beautiful flower.

♥ *Show the world your femininity and bask in the glorious feeling of being an attractive woman.*

For those of you who are squirming in your seat, I commiserate. I can assure you that I went through a long, painful phase of extreme rage against all things considered 'feminine'. Thankfully I got over it and now feel so much more comfortable in my own (female) skin. I haven't changed my attitude for men *but for the sake of my relationship with my self.* I am a woman and I have learned to be proud of that. I now enjoy playing and experimenting with things that make me feel feminine and beautiful. There is absolutely no shame in 'dressing up', or in being a woman who basks in her femininity, indeed, w*hen we reject our femininity, we reject our selves.* This is not about seeking acceptance from others *it is about embracing the Divine Feminine* of which we are all an integral part.

If you deny or reject the feminine in your self how can you expect to attract a man who will treat you like a Goddess? *Become the flower,* the Goddess, you truly are and have fun with it. Experiment and find your own style. Do what feels comfortable and attractive *to you.* If you are really estranged from your inner flower, take baby steps. Write a list of all the things you want to try or do, for your self, then do them one at a time. Pick the easiest first. Seek support from other women. If you accept your wonderful body is the Goddess incarnate, then it becomes far easier to decorate and adorn your body.

When you start to embrace your inner flower you will probably look to other women for ideas and validation. This is normal and natural;

however, it is important to avoid comparing your self to other women. Becoming the flower *is not a competition with other women*; it is an opportunity to shine in your own right. We can *all* be stunning. Each woman is different and unique in her beauty. Look to other women for support and sharing rather than to become 'better than' them. There is limitless beauty in the world and enough femininity for all of us to share. If you feel envious of other women it is a reflection of your low self-esteem, not of their being 'better' than you. Come home to your self and join forces with the rest of womankind.

I think it is worth pointing out that *becoming the flower* is definitely not about hiding your supposed 'ugliness'. Feeling driven to wear make-up or perfect clothes to avoid looking 'bad' is not the same as enjoying enhancing your body's delights. Some women won't leave the house without shaving their legs or 'putting their face on'. I am certainly not advocating this kind of thinking because it suggests that there is something wrong with you to start with and that you must therefore cover it up. Becoming the flower is about embracing your inner femininity not about 'covering up' your shameful flaws.

If you feel that you are sitting on the other side of the fence, where you use 'dressing up' to hide, then it may be worth *reducing* what you do to try and look perfect. I am not suggesting that you slum it, rather, that you let go of control so you allow yourself to learn to feel more comfortable in your own skin. Perhaps you could try leaving the house with just a bit of lip gloss and some mascara rather than making your whole face up? Perhaps you could wear jeans and trainers with a pretty top and some funky earrings? Have a go at breaking any habits you feel you *have* to do in order to merely look 'acceptable' to others.

None of these things should cost you a fortune. This is not about spending lots of money so not having a huge amount to spend should not be an excuse for not bothering. If you are on a tight budget, work out what you can do that you *can* afford rather than focusing on what you can't. My flower hair clips cost a couple of pounds and worn with my hair down *always* gets comments. You don't have to wear designer clothes to look feminine nor do you need to spend a fortune on makeup. You can have a wish list for what you want to help you become the flower and see what comes to you. Share things with friends, and/or build things up slowly if cash is tight. But if you *have* the money, go ahead and treat yourself – at least once a month.

Now you are thinking and behaving like a flower there are a few other things you can do that will help remind you that you are a beautiful flower:

- Whenever you see flowers, *notice* their stunning beauty.
- Keep fresh flowers in your home, bought or picked.
- Grow flowers in your garden or in a window box.
- Paint or buy images of flowers that you find beautiful.
- Go to a Georgia O'Keeffe exhibition or buy some prints of her work – she has got the right idea about flower energy! (I have one of her prints in a gold frame in my bedroom.)
- If you walk past flowers in the street take the time to stop and admire them, you can even smell their scent and hold their petals gently in your hand.
- Smile at the flowers to acknowledge them. You can even talk to them. (Yes, really – it won't hurt you!) Connect with their feminine energy – something you share with them. Notice the Source Energy pulsing through them. Also notice the energy of any bees buzzing around them.
- Once you have connected with the flower's Divine Feminine Energy bring the same energy home to yourself. Be reminded that you too are a wonderful flower in bloom.

♥ *Become the flower and enjoy your Divine Femininity.*

5. Invite Him In

Before you meet your Mr Wonderful, you can energetically 'invite him in' to your space. You will, of course need to know a guy is the 'real deal' before *physically* letting him into your space. When you take symbolic actions to 'invite him in' you may receive some unwanted attention. Dodgy ex- boyfriends may suddenly re-appear or want to get back into your life, which is exactly what happened to me when I did the following activities. If this happens, take it that you are being tested to see if you really are ready to let go of Mr Unavailable. The trick is to have clear boundaries in your mind *before* you begin so you don't get bowled over by the wrong guy and *not to take it personally if you manifest something you don't want*. Keep focused on what you *do want*. (Check the last chapter for advice on how to deal with an ex.)

The most effective way to invite Mr Wonderful in is by *making a space for him* and by making your home an inviting environment. This shifts your vibration and creates an energetic vacuum which the Universe will want to fill. Also, by creating space in your home you are putting your affirmations into practice which gives them powers because *actions speak louder than words*. Indeed, *any* actions you take to invite Mr Wonderful will give the Universe a strong clear message.

- **Make sure you have a double bed**. If you live in a small single room with no space for a double, it may be time to move.
- **Make sure you sleep on the left hand side of the bed**. Women who sleep on the right are unconsciously blocking male energy from coming into their space, *even when they have a partner*. Left is feminine, right is masculine – make sure you aren't inadvertently sleeping on 'his' side of the bed.
- **Get new sheets**. If you have old bedding, it may be time for some new sheets and/or a beautiful bedcover. If you haven't got the money now, save up and treat yourself.
- **Empty a drawer for him**. It doesn't have to be big, but emptying a drawer tells the Universe you want that space to be filled by a partner and creates an energetic vacuum to be filled. You can also put an affirmation, a little note or a rose quartz in the draw to help invite him.
- **If you are having a meal on your own sit at a table and lay an extra place**, as if you are expecting a visitor - *because you are!* You don't need to cook extra food, but occasionally laying a place

acknowledges to the Universe that you would like someone to eat with you.

- **Create an 'altar'.** Get two attractive candle holders and two pink or red candles. You can also use flowers, crystals, pictures that inspire you, affirmations or religious or Tantric figures to decorate your altar. Once you have built your alter you can light the candles and sit in front of it to say your affirmations, or to connect with Source. Imbue your altar with Source Energy by *using* it.

- **Do a general clutter clearing of your home.** De-cluttering is *always* a good thing to do as it clears energy and creates space. If you are not particularly tidy, it is even more important to do a clutter clear every few months. If you don't know where to start, choose one drawer, cupboard or pile that needs sorting out. Any one will do! Sort things into piles: rubbish, recycling (including charity or giving to friends), filing and keeping. Don't start clearing another drawer, cupboard or pile until you have completed the first and put everything you want to keep tidily away. Don't stop until you have completed the task at hand. Once you have put something on the rubbish pile make sure you get rid of it. If you find clutter clearing particularly challenging ask a friend to help you, or if you have the money, you can hire a life coach, or clutter clearer to take you through the process. I have discovered with clients that often it is easier than you think once you get over the procrastination.

- **Do a 'spring clean'** – even if it is November. You could even set aside a whole weekend to a big clutter clear and a spring clean.

- **Find out what the relationship corner is of your house and put a rose quartz or other love symbol in it.** If you can afford it, have your home assessed by a Feng Shui consultant. If not, you can always get some literature and have a go at it yourself or get together with some friends and have a go at doing each other's houses.

- **Clear your space of the energy of any old lovers.** Buying new sheets can help, but you can also use a smudge stick and/or a Tibetan singing bowl or a bell to clear the energy. Clear the whole house if you live alone, but if you share with others or lodge, you only need to do your own space. (Unless of course, you want to do the whole house and the people you share with don't mind.)

- **Get rid of (or put away) any old paraphernalia connected with past relationships**. If you must keep a few things, make yourself a special box and put them in there. Review the box in six months – do you still need what's in it? Sometimes it is nice to keep a few photos and love letters, but if you are holding on to a lot of stuff and/or still wearing jewellery or clothes he gave you, then you need to let go of the past to make yourself ready for a new love. Ask yourself if you need to break your tie with the past. (If you were married or your love died, then of course this process will take time. The longer you were together, the longer you need to give yourself for the process of grieving and letting go. You can do this in small, gentle stages.)

- **Make your bedroom into a gorgeous 'boudoir'**; a special place that you want to spend time in and would want to be with a partner in. Keep it tidy, put nice things in it and, if you can, change the colour scheme into something sensuous, sexy or pretty. Make it into a sanctuary and treat it as such. If all you do is sleep and/or chuck your clothes into your bedroom, or if you use it for storage, it is time to claim your sacred space back. Indulge in your bedroom – it is the closest physical space to your inner sanctum. You need to feel good in there and you want it to be a space where you would want to eventually invite a lover to join you.

♥ ♥ ♥

You now have all the tools that you will need to manifest Mr Wonderful. You have assessed where you are in relationships. You have worked on developing a relationship with yourself and Source. You have been learning strategies to raise your vibration through connection to Source, loving the self and declining negative mirrors. You have also developed new dating and manifesting techniques.

♥ *All you have to do is put what you have learned into practice.*

Chapter 6

Tending

Trusting the Process

How Can You Support the Process of Manifesting?

We have come to the final part of the journey. In this chapter you will
be given some more tools that will help you once you have got the
process under way. If you are not already dating, you can still benefit
from reading and putting into practice the following tools because they
will help wherever you are in your process.

The final part of the manifesting process involves *allowing the
Universe to deliver*. As we have already discovered, manifesting
relationships is an involved process. How you tend your garden while
you wait for things to grow (for Mr Wonderful to manifest) will make
all the difference. It is easy to get disheartened if it doesn't happen
immediately or in the manner that you expect. If this happens, it can be
tempting to throw in the towel, as I have done many times before. If
things are not unfolding the way we want or as fast as we would like
then we can become vulnerable to the temptation of Mr Unavailable or
to making short cuts which don't work out. This can all be avoided if
we know how to tend our garden while we wait for the Universe to
deliver.

Tending your Garden

There are two things to consider about gardens: Firstly, they take time
to grow. Secondly, they need regular tending. Even if you have spent
hours of backbreaking work on sorting your garden out you can't just
leave it afterwards to 'get on with it' if you don't want it to get
overgrown and strangled with weeds again. The next part of your
journey requires persistent, gentle tending. You certainly can't *make*

your garden grow; however, you *do* need to continue to give it your attention. By this stage, the hardest work may be over, but you still need to keep your garden in some kind of order and to make sure it is getting what it requires for healthy growth.

♥ *Your wonderful garden requires time, sunlight and water.*

Time

Once you have understood and started practising the skills discussed in this book, perseverance will be your greatest asset. Perseverance is a combination of commitment and patience. For some readers all you will need to do is adjust a few things, and you will be off and away. However, for many of you the process will take some time. What if you are doing all the right things and Mr Wonderful still has not arrived? And how long is this process likely to take? These are valid questions and they are certainly questions I have asked myself many times.

The more challenging your childhood and/or the bigger your sexual relationship baggage, the longer your 'growing' process is likely to take. There is no definitive guide to the time it will take because we all grow at different rates. How quickly you see results will depend on two things; how far you have to go to raise your vibration and how much effort you put in. If you have a lot of inner work to do, *this process is likely to take years rather than months.*

If you are struggling, it is not because you are being given some kind of Divine Punishment. Nor are you being treated unfairly by life, even though at times it may feel like it. All souls need challenges in order to grow and *this is the path your soul purposefully chose.* The deeper you can go with your process, the more you will learn and the more rewarding your relationship will be when you meet the right person. You are not in a race or competition with other souls. If you have relationship challenges it is not proof that you are unlovable; it is a sign that you are going through a deep energetic soul shift *which takes time and effort.*

If you are following all the guidelines outlined in this book, then you can be sure you are doing all the right things. Changing the quality of your love manifestations is like climbing a ladder. The lower down you are when you begin your journey, the further you will have to climb to get to the top. If this daunts you or causes dismay, just think about your sense of achievement when you get to where you want to be! The right relationship will come, *when you are ready*. All you can do is keep your side of the bargain by raising your vibration, practising what you have learned and by continuing to tend your garden.

♥ *Everyone's journey is unique and tailored to the individual development of their soul.*

You are a woman who wants a quality relationship that doesn't cost you emotionally. If you want any old relationship at any old price, there are *plenty* of men out there who will happily join you in the (painful) dance! If you have a long history of challenging relationships with men then it makes sense that changing the pattern *will also take time.* As long as you are learning to practice self love, you are right on track. Be patient, positive and committed to the journey and *keep tending your lovely garden.*

If you have been dating for a few months and still not met your Mr Wonderful, when should you stop trying? Well, the first thing to remember is that *you are not dating to meet Mr Wonderful*, although you may well stumble across him while you practice. A time will come when you feel you have mastered the art of being choosey because you can *easily walk away from the wrong sort of attention.* But make sure you have been able to *consistently* take care of yourself during interactions with different men. When you have reached this point you can, if you want, stop actively dating and hand the next stage of manifesting over to the Universe.

♥ *You will know when you have made the critical shift in the way you love because no matter what comes up in a date, you will have the self-esteem and confidence to deal with it in a self loving manner.*

If you lose your emotional balance and/or get confused when dating, then it is important to *continue to practice*. If the dating gets too much, you can always take a break from it for a few months. When you are rested, it is essential that you get back on the horse. Taking a rest from dating has an added benefit of giving you the opportunity to integrate what you have learned. You could try establishing a dating pattern such as six months on - six months off, or nine months on - three months off. Do what feels right for you and certainly give yourself a break when you need one.

♥ *You will need to persevere in the long run if you want to see results.*

One way that you can make your process feel less daunting is by making sure your growing garden gets plenty of sunlight and water.

Sunlight

Your garden needs sunlight to help the plants grow. Many women believe that the manifestation of the magical relationship is all that counts, and will be the only thing worth celebrating and feeling positive about. On the contrary – rather than saving the sunlight of celebration for when you manifest the relationship you really want, celebrate *all of your successes along the way*. This will give your garden the sunlight it needs and help you remain positive and motivated.

♥ *It is the journey rather than the destination that is important.*

Every small step is an achievement; every new self loving behaviour you master, every negative mirror you manage to say 'no thanks' to, and every new boundary successfully internalised. They are *all* successes, and many of them are no small feat! You could even say that mastering these challenges is reward in itself. Allow the completion of these challenging steps to give you satisfaction, *even when Mr Wonderful is nowhere in sight.*

Activity 7

You can chart your successes – the small but hugely significant personal changes you make. You can literally create a star (or other sticker) chart so you can acknowledge when you manage to do something differently. This may sound 'childish', but it really helps you to focus your efforts and to recognise what huge changes you are making. If you managed to say 'no thanks' to a one night stand when you really fancied someone, *you deserve a gold star*! Rewarding yourself for all your achievements, however small, will make the journey exciting and fun.

If you try the sticker chart, which I highly recommend, you can decide to give yourself actual rewards when you managed to get a certain number of stickers. Say £10 (or $10) per 10 stickers – or whatever you can reasonably afford. You can have different charts for different areas of development, work with different areas for improvement at different times or just have one big 'progress' wall chart.

When you earn the £10 you can either spend it on something frivolous or save it to buy something big. Put the money somewhere separate and only spend it on something you really want and really don't need. (Don't buy food or alcohol – using food or alcohol as a reward is never a good idea). You could spend it on a new lipstick, a CD, a trip to the cinema or save up for a new dress, a massage or even a beautiful sensual quilt. This not only rewards your efforts but it gives you something to look forward to when you can't see the seeds sprouting yet.

If you don't want to try the sticker chart or to buy yourself rewards you can simply journal your progress. (This is a good idea even if you also do the chart and rewards.) Buy a nice notebook especially for recording your achievements. Share them with a friend, therapist, at your women's group or with Great Spirit.

♥ ♥ ♥

When you start to see the differences in how you treat yourself and how you behave on dates you will have something solid to feel proud of. I recently had two dating experiences that mirrored two experiences I had four years ago, when I first started internet dating. (I had a lot to learn!) In both cases I handled the situation completely differently this time.

Case1: Four years ago I met a guy. I allowed him into my home, gave him my number, and allowed him to grope me in a way which felt sexual rather than romantic. I went out with him five times because he kept making the next date. I told myself he was interested, even though deep down I didn't get the feeling that he particularly liked me. I was confused when he suddenly lost interest after the fifth date (I had managed to say no to sex) and I phoned him up to ask what was going on. (Yikes!) He made some vague 'I am not sure what I want' excuse. Today I would never dream of allowing a 'date' into my home or to sexually grope me and I would never dream of calling a man who has lost interest or blown me out. However, it was this guy that made me realise that men won't get to date six unless they are genuinely inter- ested in you.

Recently I met a guy who impressed me by doing all the right 'gentlemanly' things. However, as the date progressed I began to feel that his energy was sexual rather than romantic. Even though I found him physically attractive and his kiss felt pleasant, I didn't allow myself to be flattered by his sexual attention. At the end of the date he asked me to go back to his house on the outskirts of town, to which I said 'no thanks, just take me home'. He then tried to get me to invite him into my home after I said goodbye in the car. He asked for my number, which I wouldn't give him and I decided not to see him again.

Case 2: Four years ago I met up with a guy who enthusiastically pointed out half way through the first date that it was my turn to buy a round of drinks! I was stunned, but I got up and bought him a drink and then went ahead and accepted a second date with him. On the second date he kept talking about his landlady like he was in love with her. I still agreed to a third date!

Recently I went out with a man who had agreed to pick me up on our second date. After one drink in a venue, we went somewhere else. It didn't occur to me that he was waiting for me to buy him the next drink; he just didn't seem the type. I still didn't get it even when he asked me 'are you going to get a drink?' I replied 'I'll have a white wine please...' He then curtly informed me that he wasn't going to pay for my drinks all night! This guy obviously wasn't out to impress! I was so shocked by this sudden unpleasant turn of events (I felt shamed by his comment) that I didn't know how to respond at first. After getting over the initial shock, I came to my senses. I thought 'no thanks'; this was not what I want. I wasn't going to allow a guy to shame me into buying him a drink. I turned to him and said 'Actually I am going to make a move now, see you later.' And with that I left.

You too can learn how to *handle yourself and your dates differently.* You can learn to have much higher expectations of men's behaviour toward you and you can develop the ability to say 'no thanks' and walk away. I have stopped chasing men and stopped allowing them into my space before I know I can trust them. I have walked away from several dates, which I would have been far too scared to do a few years ago. If I can do it, so can you! *And when you do, it really is worth celebrating.*

Water

In addition to sunlight, your garden also needs water. If celebration is the sunlight, spirituality is the water that sustains the growth of our garden. Connecting to Source is essential on your journey. You will need your connection to Source *even when you are deeply loved* in a committed, wonderful relationship. Source Energy is not just there for when we feel needy or because we feel something is 'missing', it is our constant energetic life line. We need Source Energy in the same way that we need water. Make sure the plants in your garden don't wilt because you have disconnected yourself from the Divine.

We can connect to Source through the practice and/or through nature, meditation, prayer or another spiritual practice that we enjoy. Find a way to connect that works for you, a way that makes you feel excited and full to the brim. Having said this, please bear in mind that you may have internal blocks to receiving spiritual succour and that you will need perseverance to get you through these barriers. Have faith that if you keep connecting to Source you will soon begin to feel the joy.

Source Energy is what we are tapping into when we manifest. It is what fills our black hole. It is who we essentially are, where we came from and where we will eventually return. It is the love we are searching for and it is always available to us even when we are not in a love relationship. Source Energy is where it is at! The more you connect to it, the higher your vibration and the greater the positive changes will be in every area of your life.

Another powerful way to connect to Source (and a good way to water your garden) is through *gratitude*. We are often encouraged as children to 'be grateful for what you have been given' when we feel resentful about something. Gratitude is not a moral 'fob off' for when you feel you are being dealt an unfair blow. It's not a case of 'be thankful for what you've got and stop complaining' because shame based gratitude is not true gratitude; it is accepting crumbs instead of expecting the cake.

♥ *True gratitude is about noticing what you already have and feeling thankful from the bottom of your heart.*

In our culture we are often highly tuned in to what is *missing* from our lives. We can easily become obsessed with trying to gain things we feel we ought to have. Heaven knows I have begrudged Source for not giving me the relationship I thought I should have, especially when I was comparing myself to others. While we are working through our process it is vital that we practice gratitude for *what we are already blessed with* because saying 'thanks' sends out powerful positive vibrations.

♥ *It really doesn't matter what entity you say 'thanks' to.*

You can show your gratitude to the sky, directly to the flowers or a friend (for being there), into your own heart, to the Earth Mother, Great Spirit, to God, Mary or Ganesh; you can say it to the Universe or to Source. You can say 'thanks' to whatever or whomever you feel personally connected to.

♥ *The important thing is that you say it and that you feel the warm flood of gratitude fill your heart.*

Saying 'thanks' has many benefits and it costs nothing, except perhaps for the gradual loss of feelings of self pity and deprivation. Gratitude helps keep things in perspective; it helps us remember that we *do have* at least some of what we want and need – and that we are already blessed. Focusing on what you have and saying 'thanks' for it raises your vibration and *opens you to receive Source Energy*.

Also, when we are in a state of gratitude we are affirming what we want to the Universe. Gratitude lets the Universe know that you want more of the same. Besides, it feels really good to focus on the blessings in your life. When you indulge in the pleasure of genuine gratitude it makes you a wonderful, positive person to be around!

Creating more gratitude

If you are used to focusing on what is missing or on what is unfair, gratitude can be a challenge. Getting into the habit of it takes practice. Try the following activities to help get you started.

Activity 8

A good way to start is to journal everything you are 'grateful' for – to list all your blessings. What is good in your life? Which people are you glad to know? What would you miss if it wasn't there? What are you taking for granted that you know other people don't have? What things do you like about yourself?

Some examples might be:

• Good health

- A wonderful home
- Having all the things you need physically
- A talent or skill
- The wonderful or fun friends in your life
- That you live on this wonderful planet

Once you have written some things down go into more detail: What specifically are you glad about with regards to your health? If you have suffered illness, you may just be glad to have survived, or to have seen an improvement in your condition. I feel grateful that I can walk after having a crippling bad back where I could barely walk for seven months. Today I feel blessed to have the freedom of being able to hike along sea cliffs and explore the countryside. I acknowledge this often and express gratitude for this incredible freedom. I could, if I was so inclined, focus on the fact that I still feel some pain and have some physical limitations because of my back condition. However, I have discovered that I would rather feel the joy and gratitude of noticing what I *can* still do, especially as I felt devastated at my loss of physical freedom when it was gone.

So, what is wonderful about your home? What do you appreciate about it? What do those wonderful friends contribute to your life? What's great about this planet? Go deeper and you will start to see how much you have, how blessed you are, even if some things in your life still need radical improvement. Remember, being positive through gratitude feels good and instantly raises your vibration because:

♥ *Focusing on what you already have creates a powerful positive vibration.*

Activity 9
Once you have done your list and gone into some detail, you can do a 'thanks-giving' ritual. You can do this alone or with friends. You can use your altar or you can make a fire outdoors, or go and find a secluded spot somewhere beautiful. Do whatever inspires you. Take your list or

write one especially for this purpose and literally say 'thank you' for each item on your list, to whomever you want to thank. Feel your heart swelling with the gratitude. I actually sometimes get tearful when I start to recognise all that I have in my life. Enjoy the natural desire within you to express gratitude.

Once you have made the initial connection with your personal expression of gratitude then you can start to make it a regular feature in your day. Saying 'thanks' isn't about being 'good' or being 'polite' it is about *recognising and honouring the bounty you are already receiving.* The bounty isn't just about material things, although that can be very important to acknowledge – it is also about love, sharing, freedom, peace and the joy of being alive. These are all things which make our lives rich. And at any time any of these things can be removed or lost, so it is important to embrace them to the full while we have them.

Activity 10

Another way to boost your positivity and to kick-start your ability to feel gratitude is to start a daily gratitude diary. Every day you have to write at least one thing that happened to you that you have gratitude for. It can be as small as noticing the amazing colours of the leaves turning in autumn or as big as a promotion at work, or meeting a wonderful person, or passing an exam. Try this for at least a week – write as many things as you can think of that felt good. Then say thanks, preferably out loud. I did this exercise for a few weeks and it completely turned my thinking around. I now notice things automatically, which is what you are aiming for.

♥ ♥ ♥

Once you are in the flow of gratitude you will start to notice as soon as something happens and say thanks in your heart, and if appropriate – out loud. Start to say 'thanks' to people, just for making you feel happy, or for sharing themselves with you. Say 'thanks' to the Universe when you see a beautiful garden, or a stunning moon. Say 'thanks' to the

Earth Mother when you tuck into a meal, or fill your fridge with yummy food. Say 'thanks' for the amazing film you have seen or the TV programme you love watching. *Recognise that what you are experiencing is a gift from the Universe.*

A close relative of gratitude, and another simple way to connect with Source, is smiling. It also costs nothing and really does make us feel better – it has been scientifically proven! When we choose to smile it becomes very hard to remain negative. So fill your life with things that make you smile. Smile at strangers on the street, and at the animals and plants you meet along the way. Smile to yourself. Smile at the Universe. Smile because you are thinking about what you have in your life; smile because you are looking forward to something next week. Enjoy the moment and enjoy being you. And smile because you have a wonderful body that allows you to experience all the pleasures of being on this planet; smile *because you can.*

Dealing with Weeds

Even with all the digging and clearing you have already done, you are still going to have weeds come up in your garden. Part of your job as the gardener is to keep the weeds at bay. A weed is simply an uninvited guest. *You get to choose what takes root in your garden* and if something is growing that you don't want, then you must remove it before it gets rooted and seeds or starts to take over.

Weeds are the relationships we don't want to get involved in. Sometimes we have to wait for a plant to grow a little before we can identify whether or not it is a 'weed'. That's why we have six dates to check our date out. Usually before the sixth date, if it is a weed we are dealing with there will be tell-tale signs. We have already covered Mr Unavailable in great detail and it is your job, as the gardener, to learn to recognise and remove Mr Unavailable from your garden before you become attached. There are, however, two other kinds of 'weed' we haven't yet discussed: the ex-boyfriend and the pseudo boyfriend.

Mr Ex

Having an ex in your life is sometimes unavoidable. However, there will be a reason the two of you broke up and it is worth remembering relationships that have been involved or sexual are *always* emotionally complicated. The most obvious time Mr Ex needs to remain part of your life is when you have children together. If this is the case then you will need to establish firm boundaries. If you still share a home with someone you are no longer 'with' it is not an excuse for maintaining a 'friendship', it is a sign that something is going on under the surface that needs to be dealt with. Ask yourself – why am I still living under the same roof with my ex? If it is only temporary, then make sure you (or he) really are making arrangements to move out.

People's relationships are complex and can break up for many reasons. However, once a relationship breaks up, it is time to move on. Trying to keep a broken relationship going on a different level (i.e.friendship) usually serves a secret emotional need for one or both parties, and is rarely healthy. The only time it is healthy to negotiate a new kind of relationship is because you need to find a way to manage still having that person in your life. Sometimes this is because of children but it may also be that you work together or that he lives in your neighbourhood or you share a circle of friends that you want to keep seeing.

If circumstances dictate that you have to keep communicating with him or seeing him, make sure that you find a way to keep your emotional distance. It is 'grown-up' to be able to smile and say hello to an ex. It isn't about being 'grown-up' when you are still going out for drinks or meals together, or having cosy chats about his new girlfriend. That is called 'remaining emotionally involved'. You can be civilised with an ex without keeping the emotional connection alive and without flirting or having sex with him. He is no longer your partner for a reason. If you were the one who let him go, why do you still want to be friends with him? If he let you go, or let you down, why would you accept his friendship in the place of his commitment to you?

There are two good reasons to weed out the ex. The first is so that you become more emotionally available for Mr Wonderful. Second and most importantly, it is to practice having healthy emotional boundaries so that your next relationship is more likely to meet your emotional needs. If you are hanging on to an ex, or allowing him to hang on to you, then you are saying 'yes please' to the Universe when you should be saying 'no thanks', *loud and clear.*

If you are finding it hard to let go, you need to identify the feelings that are keeping you stuck. If have any residue feelings of guilt, regret, fear, and/or longing then you need to work through them *without involving your ex* in the process. They are *your* feelings, so own them and deal with them. Talk to a councillor or therapist, or use your journal to work through any unresolved issues. Trying to work these feelings out by remaining emotionally involved with an ex will only keep you stuck in the negative feeling state. Remember, if you could have resolved it with him, then you wouldn't have broken up.

Be particularly wary of convincing yourself that you are remaining involved for *his* benefit. Guilt can be a powerful emotion which keeps many women attached in a 'motherly' way when what they really need to be doing is reaching out for a better relationship for themselves. Keeping the connection out of guilt won't bring you Mr Wonderful; but it *will* keep you emotionally stuck.

If you allow him to play emotional games with you or agree to have sex even though you are no longer 'together', you are saying 'yes please' to a 'don't want'. If you are missing him and enjoying seeing him socially, having a catch up cuppa with him or to the odd text exchange, it will not help you to move on – it will only keep the flame alive which makes it harder for you to have the emotional space for someone else. Hanging on to an old relationship will only ensure that you maintain your vibration in exactly the same place. It also demonstrates to the Universe that you have not yet got strong enough emotional boundaries in place to be ready for Mr Wonderful.

♥ *Boundaries with an ex are as important as boundaries with a new date and can be a real test of your commitment to change the way you love.*

If you think you two are still in love and have a chance of working things out, you can be assured that being 'pally' with him is not going to help. Take your space. Get on with your life. If he comes back to you, then things *may* have a chance of working out. If you have to keep the door open to encourage him to get back with you then you are deluding yourself and giving far too much away. *If he really loves you and wants to be with you – he will let you know.* Just like with new dates, he must be the one who does the work to get you back. Don't make it easy, put up hurdles and stick to them. And never, ever chase a man, especially not an ex who has already hurt you.

♥ *Ex-boyfriends are not the exception to the six date rule.*

Mr Ex has to make *at least* as much effort as a new guy to win your trust, *even if you both know he already has your love.* Be warned, it is much harder to have boundaries with an ex especially if there weren't any there in the first place. Putting up boundaries when you have already been sexually and/or emotionally involved is much, much harder than starting from scratch. *Don't allow yourself to underestimate how much harder it is!*

When Mr Ex wants to get back into your life then you need to be *more* cautious, and *more* convinced by his efforts. He has some serious proving to do. He has to prove that he really wants to be with you, that it isn't just convenient or easy for him. He also has to prove that things have changed or that he really wants it to work out. Mr Ex should be given the same hurdles, and you should also bear in mind that you are more emotionally vulnerable because you already have feelings for him. With an ex you already know you have something to lose because things didn't work out the first time, so it pays to make sure you really protect yourself.

You have been working at changing your own behaviour, so his interest in you may have changed. If he has noticed and likes the new you, he may become more determined to be your royal consort, and may even ask you to marry him or make another commitment. However, if he preferred you the way you were, he may be back to try and undermine your newly constructed boundaries. *Don't ever be surprised by the arrival of an ex who just wants to see if he can get away with the same thing all over again.* Exs can energetically pick up that you are trying to move on and suddenly re-appear. It is a big mistake to assume just because a guy has come back in your life that it means it is a 'fated' love. Seriously check him and his motives out before you get all starry eyed about bumping into him or getting an unexpected text.

If he treated you badly before, then the chances are he will do it again. If you are not sure about him or his intentions, you can give it a chance *but make sure you keep your boundaries;* he has to ask you out, take you out properly, and not have sex with you for at least six dates. If he doesn't pass these hurdles, he is not your Mr Wonderful. Don't go to each other's houses and you will find this a lot easier. If things haven't really changed, then it will become clear within those six dates. Make sure you keep your emotional guard up while you find out. Here are some suggestions for dealing with your ex:

♥ How to Deal With Mr Ex:

1. When communication is a necessity
2. When you are trying to be polite
3. When there is unfinished business between you
4. When you are considering responding to the advances of an ex
5. When you are still in love with him and having trouble deciding whether or not to let him go

1. When communication is a necessity

There are two types of 'ex-communications'; the sharing of important information and the exchange of emotional baggage. Sometimes it is hard to work out where the information sharing stops and the emotional baggage begins when you are communicating with an ex. If you feel confused about what is going on, then the chances are an energetic emotional exchange *is* taking place, even if nothing telling has been actually been said. Your first task is to separate the 'information' from the 'emotion'. Ask yourself the following:

- Do we actually *need* to be in contact?
- Am I communicating with my ex in order to share and/or gain specific information?

Here are some examples of legitimate topics you may need to communicate with an ex about:

- Shared childcare
- The exchange or sale of possessions
- Shared property
- Legal matters
- Medical issues (ie STIs or pregnancy)
- Shared work tasks

If you *have* to communicate with an ex, then keep your emotional and sexual boundaries. If you are discussing important issues and things feel emotionally 'messy' then take steps to protect yourself. You can employ an uninvolved third party to help such as a solicitor or mediator. Or you can use email/letters to communicate if your exchanges feel emotionally challenging. However, if you decide to write to an ex make sure you don't send any emotional outbursts, *even if you are receiving them*. Don't buy into any negativity and keep your side of the exchange as neutral as you can.

2. When you are trying to be polite
If you are in contact with an ex and it has nothing to do with the sharing of information then you have entered into the emotional realm with him. Ask yourself:

- Is one or both of you trying to be 'friendly'?

- Do you share a work place or social circle?

If you share any sort of social network it is important to remain neutral and emotionally uninvolved with an ex, regardless of any feelings you may still have about him. You can be friendly by saying 'hi' and smiling if you see him. You can even ask him how he is if you bump into him at a social event and you feel ok with this. *You don't have to exchange texts, emails, phone calls or Facebook friendship in order to remain on polite terms with an ex.*

3. When there is unfinished business between you

Sometimes there are unresolved issues and 'friendship' actually turns out to be a cover up for 'unfinished business' or an addictive relationship you can't stay away from. Ask yourself:

- Is there still an attraction between you?
- Are there any unresolved feelings between you?
- Are you missing him and wanting him back?
- Are you feeling that he still wants you?

If you openly or secretly wonder if there is still a chance that you two will 'sort things out' then you are in emotionally dangerous territory. Your previous involvement makes you extremely vulnerable and you will have to be super strong and self-aware to make sure you don't fall into bed or back into an old rut.

You could be right about him and/or your relationship – you may well be able to 'sort things out' and get back together. He may yet turn out to be 'the one' *but you will only know this for certain when he is able and willing to prove his love without any prompting or encouragement from you.* If he can't get it together to make a serious effort to sort things out then he can't possibly be your Mr Wonderful and you need to find the inner strength to say *'no thanks'*.

When there is clearly something going on and he contacts you, *you need to start from the beginning.* You don't need to tell him anything –

you just need to be clear about what it is that *you* are doing. You need to behave as if whatever you had together is now over and this is a brand new beginning that you need to make sure things get off on the right footing. When a man on a dating website only manages to send you a wink, you are supposed to ignore him because he has not made any effort. If an ex sends you a non-descript text or email, *you must also ignore it.*

Examples of a 'non-descript' message:

'I have been thinking about you'
'How are you?'
'I dreamt about you last night'
'I hope you are well'

These messages are akin to being sent a wink or a one liner from a stranger. They just don't wash. Great – so he has you on his mind. The question is; *what is he going to do about it?* An ex who lets you know that you are on his mind is usually hoping you will jump at the chance to get back with him, no questions asked. Responding to a message like this would be a seriously big mistake, especially if he didn't treat you well when you were together.

If you decide to respond to a message like this, it is because you are reading far more into it than he is actually saying. You may be tempted to interpret his message as meaning 'he loves me and wants to get back with me; we are meant to be together' when actually what he is saying is 'I'll chuck her a few crumbs hoping this will be enough to get her attention (again).' Ignore it. If he really is serious, he will find another way to reach you.

Sometimes an ex will make a little more effort and actually ask you out. However, the fact that he has asked you out is not in itself reason enough to jump straight back in. *How* he asks you out should determine whether or not he gets the pleasure of your company.

An ex is not in the position to be casual about asking you out on a date. Things didn't work out before and so special attention must be paid to getting it right this time. Some exs will be so casual when they ask you out that you will be left wondering if he actually remembers what happened between you. Here are some examples of some casual invites:

'Fancy a drink?'
'I am in the Prince of Wales, where are you?'
'I am cooking some dinner if you want to join me...'
'Wot u up 2?'
'Want to come over?'

- Casual invites are usually delivered by text, IM, email or when he bumps into you by accident.
- There is usually no reference to your past relationship or to any real feelings he has about you, though he may make a sexual overture or an offer of 'friendship'.
- The invite is designed to seem like he could just be being 'friendly' so you are left wondering whether he actually wants to get back with you.
- It will often require an immediate response because it is a last minute invite.

Casual invites from an ex are no better than an 'I've been thinking about you' message. Causal invites require little or no effort on his part and their ambiguity is emotionally confusing. A woman with low self-esteem will often jump at the chance to see him again, just so she can convince him she is still interested and worth his meagre attention. On the other hand, a woman with high self-esteem will see that he is offering her *absolutely nothing* and his invite does not deserve *any* response, not even an angry one. Ignore it!

4. When you are considering responding to the advances of an ex

Sometimes a man will realise that he has made a mistake in letting you go. Sometimes a man realises that you are the one for him after you have broken up. You may decide an ex deserves another chance when you can see he is making an effort and that things have changed. Whatever happens, *it is crucial that you take things very slowly and don't make any promises until you know for sure that things are different.* You must never re-enter a broken relationship in order to prove that you are lovable. You can re-enter a relationship if he proves to you that he is ready to give you what you deserve. To know this for sure requires *evidence.*

♥ *Growth in a relationship requires the full commitment of both parties.*

You will know that your man is ready to love you when he demonstrates to you that he can:

1. Acknowledge and calmly express his feelings to you
2. Listen carefully to you and accept your feelings
3. Take responsibility for his part in what went wrong
4. Make amends for any harm he has caused you
5. Reach a suitable resolution with you
6. Make a sustained effort to win your trust
7. Be absolutely clear about his intentions toward you
8. Put his words and promises into *consistently reliable* action
9. Demonstrate his commitment to you and to working things out
10. Show he is fully emotionally available for you *today*

Of course *you also need to be able to do all of the above* and if you can't, then it is time to focus on working on your own relationship skills rather than trying to hash out a failed relationship. However, if in the past you have been the one trying to make things work, or if you have been trying to get him to change or to treat you properly, then he will need to meet *all* of the above criteria before you even consider getting involved with him again. If he can't demonstrate the above criteria then he simply hasn't grown enough to start giving you what you deserve. You will end up in a repeat performance which will only serve to lower your vibration. Your ex may well love you but if he doesn't have these relationship skills or show a commitment to working on them, then he is not your Mr Wonderful, he is Mr Unavailable with roots growing deep in your garden. Dig them out!

5. When you are still in love with him and having trouble deciding whether or not to let him go

It is important not to beat yourself up for still having feelings for an ex, especially when you are dealing with relationship addiction. You really cannot help the way you feel. You may still really love him and hope that it works out. You may miss him and wish things could be different. But we have no control over our past, or over the emotional attachments that were made. It is not helpful to try and make yourself 'get over' someone or change your feelings about them. All you can do is keep reminding yourself that *if it is supposed to work out with him, then he will find a way to win your trust and make it work without any encouragement from you.* If he doesn't, then you will find a way to move on, even if it takes time. It is worth noting that sometimes it takes falling in love with someone new to fully let go of and old love, *and that is ok.*

♥ *You don't have to stop having feelings for an ex in order to manifest Mr Wonderful, but you absolutely must disengage from the emotional involvement.*

While we have no control over our *feelings*, we do have control over our *actions*. We can choose to:

• Protect ourselves by only having essential or unavoidable contact
• Avoid emotionally/sexually charged or ambiguous exchanges
• Take responsibility for owning and processing all of our feelings *without involving our ex partner.*
• Refuse to respond to 'I've been thinking about you' messages
• Ignore 'casual invitations' to meet up

If you are still not sure what to do about an ex, then this imaginary scenario may help you decide:

Imagine that you are on a mission to get to the top of High Vibration Mountain. You have successfully negotiated your way across a treacherous river. Your journey has taken you further up stream where a path to the mountain has finally been revealed. You are feeling really excited about your progress and just as you are about to head off up the new path your ex suddenly appears, frantically waving to you from the other side of the river. He seems to want you again and he is pulling at your heart strings.

If your ex has appeared on the other side of the river, waving to get your attention, it either means that he is ready to join you on your journey or that you are being tested to see how much you want to get to High Vibration Mountain. Your job is to work out whether it is a genuine offer of love or a test of your resolve to walk away and thus raise your vibration. If all he is doing is waving or calling you from the other side (i.e. sending 'I am thinking about you' messages or 'casual invitations'), then it is likely that he is hoping that you will abandon your mission and go back to be with him. If this is the case you can respond in several ways:

1. You can decide to go back to where you came from and stay with him instead of continuing on your journey to High Vibration Mountain or...
2. You can put your mission on hold while you put all your energy into trying to get him to cross the river by instructing him on what he needs to do, or on trying to build a bridge for him to cross or...
3. You can smile as you continue on your path to High Vibration Mountain, trusting that if he is truly the one for you, *he will find a way to cross the river and join you on your journey.*

♥ ♥ ♥

If he is your Mr Wonderful you can be completely confident that *he will rise to the challenge.* If he is not your man, then you are simply being tested by the Universe. Are you really ready to move on? Are you up to the task of climbing High Vibration Mountain? You can be absolutely sure that your path to the mountain will be blocked until you successfully pass this test. *And you are highly likely to be tested if you still have strong feelings for an ex.* Whether or not you can 'pass' depends entirely on whether or not you are ready to walk on, *despite your feelings for him.* It is our feelings that can keep us stuck and we have to willing to rise above them if we want to raise our vibration.

There is only one way to find out if your ex is ready to join you on the journey to High Vibration Mountain. *He will have to find a way to cross the river to get to you.* He must be willing to either get wet, find stepping stones, make a little bridge or to find a boat. How he gets across is entirely up to him but unless you see him making a serious effort to find a way without any instructions from you, then you must continue on your journey without him, that is, unless you want to stay exactly where you are and experience more of the same.

Your ex may be ready to climb High Vibration Mountain with you if he makes an effort to:

- Ask you out *properly* (makes proper contact with you and pre-plan the date, etc)
- Make his intentions clear
- Let you know that he wants to talk things over
- Let you know how he feels about you
- Make any amends that are due
- Offer to try and find a solution with you

Telling you that he misses you and wants to get back together *is a start.* Then you need to see that he also has the emotional maturity to take responsibility for the way things went and to make amends for any harm he may have caused you. And, even if he says sorry, that may *still* not be enough – especially if you had to prompt him. He needs to be able to come up with a resolution that will work for both of you and you need time to see if what he proposes works. You will also need to check that his words are followed by consistent actions.

Obviously every man is different and you will know in your heart if he is doing things differently or not. If he rarely expresses how he feels and then he sends you a text to say that he misses you, wait a couple of days and then text back saying you miss him too, *but that is all*. Don't respond to a text like this more than once. If he sends you flowers or a card for the first time, cut him a little slack, even if he doesn't spell things out instantly. On the other hand if you are tired of hearing the same old apologies, wait to see if he offers a solution to how you can move forward before seeing him again. The key to knowing whether a man really is making an effort is when you see him step outside of his comfort zone and he shows he is willing to do *whatever it takes*.

♥ *You need to give yourself plenty of time to see if you can trust him to love you the way you deserve to be loved.*

Until you are sure you can trust him, it is crucially important not to have any sexual relations with him and not to make any commitments or promises. If you sleep with him or make promises you will find it much harder to stick to your guns. If you know you will not be able to avoid having sex with him, take this as an indicator of how much power you are currently giving to him, and how risky seeing him will be. *If he wants to make it work he will wait.* If he can't wait, then he simply isn't your Mr Wonderful and it is time to move on, whatever your feelings.

If you discover you can't yet walk away even though in your heart you know that you should, don't beat yourself up about it. Your journey is a process and *inner growth takes time*. Trust that if you keep focusing your energy on raising your self-esteem and on developing self loving behaviours, in time you will find the inner strength to do what is best for you. Until then, the most self loving thing to do is to seek additional support. (See the appendix for suggestions.)

Mr Pseudo Boyfriend

You see this guy as your 'best friend' and/or you spend loads of time 'hanging out' together. You probably have deep and meaningful talks with him and are quite happy going to the cinema, out for a cosy meal, or even cuddling and being affectionate with him. Perhaps you can share shoulder rubs and talk about past relationships with him or even sleep in the same bed but for some reason it never goes beyond 'friendship'. There are several possible reasons for this.

1. He doesn't really fancy you
2. You don't really fancy him
3. One or both of you isn't emotionally ready for a genuine committed relationship
4. One of you is involved with someone else

This is what I call a 'pseudo relationship': an emotionally bonded, intense, close 'friendship' with a man who acts as a 'stand-in' boyfriend.

Sometimes things do get sexual with Mr Pseudo Boyfriend, but you decide to remain 'friends'. Other times the sexual side is completely sublimated or denied in one or both parties. Sometimes one of you is already in a relationship with someone else and doesn't want to 'cheat' so won't allow things to develop sexually to avoid feeling guilty (this is of course being emotionally unfaithful). Usually their other relationship is struggling or close to ending and they are looking for emotional succour or the next relationship to jump into.

Whatever the underlying dynamic, pseudo relationships are always about trying to meet emotional needs without being emotionally honest and/or committed. Pseudo relationships are marked by a lack of emotional and/or sexual boundaries and denial or confusion about the true nature of the relationship. Invariably at least one person is secretly being hurt or disappointed by the pseudo relationship, even if it is a third party. However, sometimes it seems to suit both parties to settle for an emotionally intense relationship without the commitment or the sex; that is until one person finds a real relationship and leaves the other one high and dry.

If you have a 'pseudo boyfriend' who you do not fancy, chances are he secretly fancies you and he is hoping things will change. You are potentially leading him on if you have no intention of allowing things to develop.

If you have a P.B. that you secretly fancy and hope will make a move on you then you are setting yourself up to get hurt. (If he really does want you he is more likely to realise this if you keep your emotional distance *and you need to keep that distance to protect yourself.*)

If you have a P.B. that is otherwise involved, you are not only hurting yourself but are party to hurting their partner, which means you are vibrating at a very low level indeed. It is time to wake up and smell the coffee. He is not available and your relationship is inappropriate. Just because there is not sex involved doesn't make it 'ok'.

If both of you just like hanging out with each other and you really think neither of you is getting 'led on' then having a pseudo boyfriend is still a bad idea. If one of you finds a partner, the other is likely to get hurt and more importantly, if you are hooked up on a pseudo relationship, you are not emotionally available for Mr Wonderful. The relationship is not meeting all your needs so it is a 'don't want' – a weed that needs to be pulled up and put in the compost bin. By getting emotionally involved in a pseudo relationship you are saying 'yes please' to a 'don't want' and telling the Universe that this is all you want. If you must remain friends, work on creating emotional boundaries and keeping your distance.

Of course men and women can be 'friends'. It is however rare that in a close friendship between a hetero man and woman that one or other party isn't sexually interested, even if they accept that the other party doesn't feel the same. Friendship between men and women needs to have strong boundaries because of the natural sexual element between them. Having good male friends in a group is very different from having regular intimate 'one to ones' with a guy. If you like him, and he only seems to want to be friends, then hanging out with him all the time is not going to encourage him to take things to the next level. Get choosey! Your not being hyper available to him may make him realise that he really wants to be with you. On the other hand he may just be Mr Mixed Messages in the guise of a friend.

♥ ♥ ♥

Whether you are meeting new men or have a few old ones still hanging around, it is important to keep the 'weeds' at bay in your garden. Remember, a weed is simply a relationship 'don't want'. As soon as you realise that you are getting involved in an emotional 'no win' situation, it is time to disengage. It may seem ruthless or heartless at first, but you will soon discover that keeping the weeds out it is about being emotionally safe and raising your vibration.

Having a weed free garden will enable your energetic vibration to continue climbing up the ladder and you will realise that you don't actually need those emotional involvements that don't give you what you want and deserve.

The Space In Between

So, you have decided that after years of painful or disappointing relationships you are going to stop going out with unavailable men. You decide to start with a clean slate. You have learned what to look out for – what the signs of Mr Unavailable are. You have a better understanding about why you choose people who don't love you back. Perhaps you have also had some counselling and this time you know you are ready to break the pattern. You know you must 'create a space' to invite a new type of relationship into your life. Great! You picture clearing a space and some great new available lover coming to meet you... and then what, *nothing?*

All your old relationships are tied up. You know what the problems were and you know there is nothing more you can do, except wait for something new. Your journey has brought you to be able to let go of an old way of being, to break a pattern or a habit. When you have decided not to 'pick up' that old familiar behaviour again, you will be faced with the *Space In Between*.

Many people try to avoid this stage. Putting something down is one thing. Deciding not to pick it up again, even when there is nothing else in you hand to distract you is quite another. It is often this stage that sends us running into the arms of an old or new Mr Unavailable. Some of us may try and avoid this by lining someone up before we make any changes; for example, a new lover is found and secured before the old is left or we run into the arms of an ex or a pseudo boyfriend. Yet the *Space In Between* stage is designed to be tough and we are *supposed* to be tested.

♥ *Our soul is always asked 'are you really ready to change?'*

This stage reminds me of the challenging rite of passage many spiritual seekers are faced with. When we are ready to transform our old ways, we are often mercilessly tempted. It feels like pure torture and we wonder what sort of God (or Life) would be so cruel to test our strength when we are at our most vulnerable. It is not, however, a test of our moral fabric to see if we are 'good or bad'. *We are being tested to see if we are truly ready for the next stage in our soul's development*; are we ready to raise our vibration and move up the relationship ladder? There are no moral judgements here, just a need to check for your absolute commitment to do whatever it takes.

♥ *If you slip back or get stuck, you are simply not ready.*

This kind of challenge is a *soul transition* because we are leaving something behind or changing something that we have been very attached to over a period of time, possibly even lifetimes (if you believe in that). A soul transition is all about deep growth and it affects us on a profound level. It is a right of passage, and therefore it has important stages. The *Space In Between* stage is the final part when our soul is tested to see if we really *are* resolved to move up a level, or to break a pattern of behaviour that is not in our best interest. Soul transitions are not to be taken lightly. If you try and skirt over this important stage, then you are bound to get caught short by whatever you are trying to 'give up', change or leave behind.

While in the *Space In Between*, when we are waiting for our new garden to grow, we have to face our fears. We have said 'not any more' to something but then we are faced with the scary space of 'not having' and all our feelings start to surface. This is actually a very fertile stage in our development. Our deeper self will surface and all that we have been trying to hide from will suddenly surface. We may feel more empty, lonely or scared. What if nothing will come to replace the old? What if this is all there is? 'Surely', we convince ourselves, 'it is better to have the old thing we want to let go of than deal with this *nothingness.*'

Imagine you have an over grown garden that is full of weeds and brambles. You decide enough is enough – it's time to sort it out – you want a beautiful garden full of flowers or maybe to grow your own vegetables or fruit trees. So you start to cut down the vines, slash the nettles and tackle the brambles with sheers. It is hard work but you can really get your teeth into it. You can also see what you are dealing with. Sweat and tears and a sense of purpose; this is the satisfying bit. Each day you can see how well you have done, and how much is left to do. There is a clear light at the end of the tunnel. This is akin to getting rid of the dead wood in your life – the relationships, activities or behaviours that don't work.

Then you prepare the soil. You dig, add manure and air it to make it ready for planting. You transform the ground to create a space for something new to grow. Next you carefully plant your seeds and you stand back and look at your garden, satisfied with all the work you have done. Then, all of a sudden, all you can see is the soil, *the exposed earth*. Your garden feels empty and you become profoundly aware that you do not actually have the end result for all your hard work. You didn't expend all that energy to end up with an empty garden!

Yes, the weeds have gone, but there is also an absence of flowers, veg or fruit growing. It would be nice if the next day you woke up and your new garden had appeared, ready to greet you – but no; it looks as bare as it did the day before. In a few days some weeds may have taken root again and you have to go back and pull them out. This is what the *Space In Between* is like. It is a no man's land and it can be very frightening or confusing when we reach this stage in our life. That's exactly when the dreaded 'what ifs' and other self-sabotaging doubts can start to emerge from the recesses of our minds.

At this moment we often feel exposed and what we are trying to leave behind often comes back to check if we are serious. Just like weeds. Their seeds are still held in the soil and they will grow back. It would really be quite odd if they didn't. So what would you say to a gardener who saw a few weeds growing back after digging up a whole garden and said:

'Oh well, perhaps this garden is supposed to have weeds in it. The other plants haven't grown. Maybe they are not coming after all. (Deep sigh.) I can't stand this empty garden it seems so, so bare – I think I'll just let the weeds grow back. Maybe I will get rid of them when I see my flowers growing or my trees fruiting. I mean how do I know if the seeds I planted will ever grow? I don't want to take that risk.'

Would you respond by saying *'Gardener, you are right! It's too much of a risk and a bare garden is really bad. Let the weeds grow and cover that soil.'* Or would you say *'Gardener – you have just done all that work and now you have to be patient and have faith. Your seeds will grow and what you need to do now is tend your garden and KEEP THE WEEDS OUT! It takes longer to grow vegetables and flowers and fruit than it does to let the weeds take hold. Hang in there and watch what happens – It really is magic!'*

It sounds obvious when we think about gardens but saying 'no thanks' to inappropriate lovers before we have found the right person is incredibly hard, especially if our garden has been bare for sometime. Saying 'no thanks' to a pseudo boyfriend you know isn't ultimately good for you when you haven't got anything else lined up can seem impossible or even hard hearted. Saying 'no thanks' to an ex who wants to sleep with you, exchange texts or get back into the old groove with you can seem like a fate worse than death because you are dealing with giving up something you once wanted *and* not having anything to fill the hole that is left.

♥ *Saying 'no thanks' to distractions and temptations is exactly what is required of you during the Space In Between.*

Because we cannot see how things are going to turn out, it feels hard to let go. But we must stand fast if we are to get the results we want. It takes time to grow and nurture a garden. It takes time to develop new relationships and self loving behaviours. Sometimes we have to just live with the gap that is left when we have let go of the old. One thing you can be sure of is that this stage won't last forever. And this gap is there precisely to challenge as we are thrown into that confusing or painful place. The question is; how will we respond? Will we throw in the towel or will we embrace the challenge? Well, if you decide that you want to embrace the challenge then here's how...

♥ **How to Manage the 'Space In Between':**
1. Accept the process.
2. Commit to the process.
3. Keep pulling the weeds out.
4. Remember to keep watering your garden and letting the sunlight in.

1. Accept the process
You are making a *soul transition* and so you are highly likely to experience the Space In Between. There will be, at the very least, an adjustment period when things feel strange and awkward. When you get there, you can see it for what it is and allow this part of the process to take as long as it takes. It may be days, it may even be years, but accept it for what it is – a vital stage in your soul's growth, and if you find yourself there it is a really good sign that you are undergoing some deep soul growth, which is something to feel proud of.

2. Commit to the process

If you give up at this stage then your garden will revert to the bramble jungle you so painstakingly tackled. Of course, you can always go back to clearing it again in the future but you will still have to face the Space In Between at *some* point. If the time isn't right for you yet, then so be it, but don't fool yourself into thinking that the 'right time' will be when you find a way to skip this stage of the process. Ask yourself honestly, how would your soul grow if you could orchestrate a transition while skipping this strengthening phase?

If you find that you have fallen into a long term pattern of clearing and then giving up, you may find the whole soul transition process feels very futile and punishing. Sitting with the Space In Between when you have been in the pattern for a while may be even *more* of a challenge because you've worked so hard for so long without having ever experienced any real results, which is of course very disheartening. This can make the bare soil seem even more ominous as you lament 'what's the point – I have done so much already and it has never made any difference before.' So, decide to stick with it *this* time, and give your soul a chance to move on. If you really don't believe it will work – *act as if you think it will work.*

♥ *Give the Universe a chance to do its magic before you make your final judgement.*

3. Keep pulling the weeds out

Weeds are the unwanted influences that will drain, strangle or take over your garden if you let them, without bearing any fruit. Remove the destructive and when it tries to return, remove it again. Be ruthless. When a weed comes in a new guise, don't be fooled. A weed is a weed – if it's not what you planted, it's not going to help you and it will only get in the way. Don't be tempted to waste your energy nurturing weeds or even just allowing them to quietly reside in your garden. If you do let a weed grow, before long you will be back where you started. If you are not sure if a relationship with a guy is a 'weed' or not, give him the six date challenge.

4. Remember to keep watering your garden and letting the sunlight in

This will help you to clear your mind of all the doubt and fear and will help you to 'sit with' the awkward or challenging Space In Between. Allow yourself to feel all the feelings that surface in this stage and then let them go. It is important to face your fears but do not allow them to take root and tempt you into abandoning your beautiful garden.

♥ *When we decide to continue nurturing our garden even when it seems bare, our fears can be transformed into an excited anticipation.*

Ultimately the Space In Between prompts us to develop our trust in our inner growth process and our ability to allow the Universe to deliver, *in its own good time*. Like with a garden, our soul's growth begins under the surface where we can't see it. Your soul's purpose is *always* to grow, so trust that when you are ready for the challenge of a committed loving relationship, you will receive what you need to make this happen and Mr Wonderful will appear in your life.

When you demonstrate to the Universe that you are ready for the next stage in your development, new bright green shoots will begin to appear in your garden. And you will know instinctively that the tender little shoots are not the weeds returning: They are the budding of a loving relationship that you want to stay in *because it feels wonderful.*

Appendix

Useful Resources

- Recommended reading
- Self reflection tools
- 12 Step support groups
- Counselling and therapy
- Coaching
- Singles support groups

Recommended Reading

There are many great books available on the subject of personal and spiritual growth. I have provided a list of books which I have personally found to be the most inspiring and supportive.

Dating, Men and Women:

> *The Surrendered Wife* (Pocket Books, new edition 2006)
> *The Surrendered Single* (Pocket Books, new edition 2006)
> Laura Doyle

These two books present a revolutionary approach to love relationships. Originally writing for married women, Laura's first book *The Surrendered Wife* contains all the rationale behind Laura's 'no control' approach to dealing with men. These two books will give you plenty of reasons to allow men to take care of you without having to hand over your power. *The Surrendered Single* was written in response to the many women who had loved her first book but had not yet found their 'good guy'. There are many useful dating tips in her second book.

> *The Rules for Online Dating* (Pocket Books, 2002)
> *The Complete Book of Rules* (Harper Element, 2000)
> Ellen Fein and Sherrie Schneider

Originally I didn't 'get' *The Rules* – at first glance they seemed to me to be gamey and perhaps insincere. However, when I applied their online dating strategies, I found the rules approach really helped and covered most dating situations. If you follow their advice you will save yourself a lot of time and heartache. You are actively encouraged to not make your self too available when dating men. These books will remind you how important it is to become *choosey* when looking for a mate.

> *Men are from Mars, Women are from Venus* (Thorsons, new edition 2002)
> *Mars and Venus on a Date* (Vermillion, 2003) John Gray

It is great to hear about dating from a male perspective. John Gray has highlighted just how different men and women are emotionally and how we need to consider this fact when relating to the opposite sex. His first book *Men are from Mars, Women are from Venus* really is an enlightening read which will give you plenty to think about, that is if you haven't already read it! *Mars and Venus on a Date* applies the same principles to dating – definitely worth a read, if only to hear a man explain the way men think.

Manifesting and Spiritual Growth:

> *Stepping in the Magic* (Piatkus Books, new edition 1995)
> *Living Magically* (Piatkus Books, new edition 1995)
> Gill Edwards

Gill Edwards was responsible for opening my eyes to a whole new way of seeing the world. These books will introduce you to many spiritual tools and ideas that will change the way you think. Her books demonstrate that there is no such thing as a coincidence, that we are being guided by Source all the time. We just need to learn how to read the signs.

Ask and it is Given (Hay House, 2006)
Esther and Jerry Hicks

This book contains the channelled teachings of Abraham. *Ask and it is Given* is both practical and inspiring. It goes into great detail about the process of manifesting and reveals the vibrational scale of human emotions.

Excuse Me, Your Life is Waiting (Mobius, 2005)
Lynn Grabhorn

Lynn Grabhorn explains the art of manifesting in an accessible style. *Excuse me, your Life is Waiting* explains the crucial emotional aspect of manifesting and the importance of focusing on 'wants' rather than 'don't wants' – something we often forget to do.

Why Me, Why This, Why Now? (Arrow Books, 1995)
Robin Norwood

The author of *Women Who Love Too Much* (see below) also wrote this amazing book about the spiritual process of human development. It covers karma and soulmates and explains the deeper meaning to our lives and loves.

Creative Visualisation (Transition Vendor, new edition 2002)
Living in the Light (Transition Vendor, 1998)
Skakti Gawain

Both these books offer a very good introduction to manifesting and the incredible power of creative visualisation.

Women Who Run With the Wolves (Random House Publishing Group, 1996)
Clarissa Pinkola Estes

This is a delightful and thought provoking book. Pinkola Estes provides deep insights into the soul life of women using the psychological interpretation of popular fairy tales from around the world. Myths can offer us pathways into the world of the psyche and she guides her readers on a beautiful journey towards feminine empowerment.

Emotional Healing:

> *Women Who Love Too Much* (Arrow, new Ed 2004)
> *Letters from Women Who Love Too Much* (Arrow, 1989)
> Robin Norwood

Women Who Love Too Much is a life changing book which deals with damaging relationships between men and women. This was the book which started me on my own journey of self discovery, back in 1989. If you have issues with addictive or abusive relationships you will find these two books offer a clear explanation of the nature of these destructive relationships, while also offering a strong message of hope and recovery. A must read if you find yourself undeniably stuck with Mr Unavailable.

> *Codependent No More* (Hazelden, 1989)
> *The Language of Letting Go* (Hazelden, 1990)
> Melody Beattie

Melody is a leading author on the subject of codependency. She covers topics such as boundaries, detachment and meeting our own needs in a clear and accessible manner. Both books are a 'must read' for all who struggle to keep their boundaries.

The Language of Letting Go is a wonderful book of daily meditations encouraging good self-care. If you have any problems in this area, then this book will be a great additional daily support.

The Courage to Heal (Vermillion 1997)
Ellen Bass and Laura Davis

Many women were sexually abused during childhood and/or adolescence. If you were or think you may have been abused, then this book will be a great help. It has been called 'the survivor's bible' as it is packed full of information, personal stories and tools for dealing with this extremely common (and deeply challenging) problem. If you want to create better relationships and sexual abuse has been an issue for you, then *The Courage to Heal* really is an essential resource.

Self Reflective Tools

There are many different tools available to us which we can use to help us develop our self-awareness. People often believe that divinatory tools such as tarot cards, astrology and rune stones are used for 'fortune telling'. Many people do learn to use them for this purpose, yet divinatory systems can also be used for self reflection and are also a powerful method for connecting to Source.

My personal journey of self reflection began with astrology and tarot when I was around fifteen years old. I have worked with many systems since then and have found the following divinatory cards to be both accessible and effective tools.

It is suggested that you only work with one set of cards at a time. A good way to start using them is by picking one card for daily reflection. Once you feel familiar with the cards and their meanings, then you can develop other methods of use or try out another set if you wish.

Medicine Cards by Jamie Sams and David Carson
(Bear and Company, 1988)
The Discovery of Power through the Ways of Animals

Sacred Path Cards by Jamie Sams
(HarperSanFransisco, 1990)
The Discovery of Self through Native Teachings

Osho Zen Tarot by Osho
(Gateway1994)
The Transcendental Game of Zen

Motherpeace Tarot by Vicki Nobel and Karen Vogel
(US Games Systems, Inc, 1995)
A Way to the Goddess through Myth, Art and Tarot

The Goddess Oracle by Amy Sophia Marashinsky
(Element, 1997)
A Way to Wholeness through the Goddess and Ritual

The Crystal Ally Cards by Naisha Ahsian
(Heaven and Earth Publishing, 1995)
The Crystal Path to Self Knowledge

12 Step Fellowships

(The following information is based purely on my personal under-standing and experience.)

12 Step fellowships offer recovery from addictions and other dysfunctional behaviours. There are many 'sister' fellowships that use the 12 Step recovery programme pioneered by Alcoholics Anonymous (AA). You can find fellowships which deal with a whole host of issues including drugs, growing up in an alcoholic family, sex (addiction), co-dependency and eating disorders.

The 12 Steps are a tried and tested method for overcoming unman-ageable and destructive behaviours in ourselves, including our addic-tions. There are many advantages to 12 Step meetings:

- There is no fee (donations are collected at all meetings to cover costs)
- The meetings are organised by people who are also recovering from the same issue; support is peer-based rather than 'professional'
- Fellowships are led by consensus from the grass roots rather than by

powerful people at the top

- You can go along to a meeting and just listen – your active participation is not required
- All the people there will know what you feel like and will find identification with what you say if you decide to share
- The 12 Steps are a tried and tested method of healing that was established over 50 years ago and has undoubtedly improved and saved many lives
- The fellowship offers an empowering 'spiritual solution' without religious affiliation

If you know (or suspect) you are struggling with an addiction or you recognise yourself as being a 'love addict' or codependent, it is well worth seeking the unconditional support and guidance found in 12 Step meetings. You can search the internet to find a fellowship that suits you.

Once you have located the relevant fellowship, you can find out if there are any meetings in your area. If you can't find exactly what you are looking for, it is worth going to a different fellowship that deals with a similar or related problem. If all else fails you can go to an 'open' AA meeting where you don't need to be an alcoholic to attend. When it comes to healing and recovery, it is always better to try *something* rather than doing nothing at all.

It is worth noting that not all 12 Step fellowships are as well established as AA and not *all* meetings are healthy. It is the same as anything – where there are humans involved there is imperfection! If you find a meeting where members are not working the 12 Steps (in sponsorship) or sticking to (or even mentioning) the 12 Traditions, then be aware that the meeting is only doing the first half of the process – *identifying the problem*. You need a meeting that is also *working the solution*. This is unlikely to happen in well established fellowships such as AA or NA (Narcotics Anonymous) but it can, and does happen in other fellowships. If you find yourself in a meeting that is not 'solution based' you have several options; you can:

- Look for another meeting in the same fellowship;
- Try another related fellowship
- Stay in the meeting and get a sponsor from a more established fellowship (or meeting) so that you can get the guidance you need to work the steps and traditions.

It is possible to receive long distance sponsorship, I have even known of people with sponsors in other countries. Support and identification with others who share the same problem(s) is a very important part of the healing process but ultimately the solution lies in working the 12 Steps and in adhering to the 12 Traditions.

If you are a newcomer who is not entirely happy with the meeting you are attending, you would be better off finding a new meeting, fellowship or a sponsor from outside the group rather than trying to change things from within. Once you are well established in your own recovery you may be able to help your meeting get back on track.

♥ *If you truly want to get well, Source will help you find a way.*

Alcoholics Anonymous
www.aa.org
www.alcoholics-annonymous.org.uk

Coda (Co-dependents Anonymous)
www.codependents.org
www.coda-uk.org

Over Eaters Anonymous (for eating disorders)
www.oa.org
www.oagb.org.uk

Counselling and Therapy

There are many varieties of counselling and therapy available and many different avenues for getting such support. Ultimately it comes down to personal choice. However, I can make some suggestions that may make choosing a counsellor or therapist a little easier.

As a rule of thumb, it is important to shop around. Taking the first therapist you come across is like choosing to marry the first guy who asks you out or buying the first house you see that has a 'for sale' sign. You *may* get lucky but equally, you may not and you won't know unless you take the time and effort to check things out.

Seeing an advert and getting an appointment does not mean you have found the right practitioner, it simply means that you have found a *potential* practitioner. (Does this sound familiar?) I would suggest you go and meet *at least* three practitioners before making your final choice. You may have an initial interview, or perhaps an introductory session; however, a phone call is not enough to decide whether the practitioner is right for you – you need to meet them in person.

Things to consider before approaching a practitioner:

- Do you want a male or female practitioner or are you open to either?
- Would you prefer a counsellor (someone to just listen) or a therapist (someone who is more probing)?
- What can you afford?
- Do you need to ask for concessions?
- Do you want weekly or fortnightly sessions?
- Would you like an ongoing arrangement, or a set number of sessions?

When you go for your first appointment it is worth getting prepared. You can even write your questions down if it helps. Remember, you are interviewing them for a very important job and you have every right to ask questions. A good practitioner will not be concerned or upset by this mature approach. You need to find out the following:

- Are they offering the kind of therapy you want? If you are not sure, ask them to explain their approach and its benefits. It may be worth seeing practitioners with different approaches to help you decide the right method for you.

- Are they qualified to practice and professionally registered? (You may also want to know if they are insured.)
- Do they feel comfortable and qualified to work on the issues you want to discuss?
- Are they comfortable with helping you set goals and reviews? It is a good idea to have some goals that you are working towards so you can see if you are making progress. If you are not sure what your goals might be then the practitioner should be able to help you decide and be able to offer regular review sessions.
- Can they offer you a regular slot at a time that is convenient for you?

While you are having your introductory session you need to also ask *yourself*:

- Do I feel comfortable with this person?
- Do they make me feel safe?
- Do they seem to like me?
- Do I like them?
- Do they seem to have good personal boundaries?
- Are they clear and straightforward in their manner?
- Do they have good time keeping? (This will give you a good indicator of their boundaries)

You may want to journal answers to these questions when you get home. Like when you go on a date, *always* trust your feelings. If you don't feel comfortable, safe or liked, then you are wasting your time and money because the practitioner can't possibly help you. There must be a mutual rapport between you for there to be any real benefit, which is why shopping around is essential.

Once in therapy, you can always change your mind. Just because you have agreed to work with a practitioner doesn't mean you can't change your mind if you find that you don't really work well together after all. You may need more than one session to get a really good feel for the way the practitioner works. If it takes a while to realise that actually the answer to any of the above questions is 'no' then you have every right to find someone else to work with.

If you have issues with sexual boundaries or have a history of abusive relationships with men, it is a good idea to start your healing process with a woman practitioner. It can be unnecessarily confusing to work with a man when you have been abused by one, especially very early on in your process.

It is also important to note that it is possible to attract abuse in therapeutic situations. Just because someone is a qualified therapist does not automatically mean they are 'safe' or 'right'. If you have any doubts about a therapist's behaviour or conduct, make sure you talk to someone *other* than the therapist before deciding what to do. Always trust your instincts, especially if you are feeling confused. There are professional bodies set up to deal with such issues, so make sure you seek good advice before taking any action.

Once you have the right practitioner, the support and insight you will gain can be an enormous benefit. It really is worth taking the effort to find the right person and the right method for you.

Relationship Coaching

Coaching has become very popular in recent years and it can be a very powerful way to get things moving in your life. If you feel that you do not need the level of emotional support offered in therapy/counselling but you would like someone on your side who can keep you focused on your relationship goals, then a coach may be just what you are looking for. If you know you have emotional issues to work through, then you would be better off going for therapy/counselling first. If you are ready for action, then go for coaching!

A good coach will:

- Be qualified by a reputable and well recognised teaching body
- Make you feel listened to, understood, liked and respected
- Elicit your needs and goals and guide you rather than setting their

own agenda
- Draw out your inner answers and make additional suggestions rather than simply telling you what to do
- Make sure the sessions are highly focused, goal-oriented and effective
- Give you plenty of encouragement, support, validation and feedback
- Make sure you have an 'action plan' by the end of each session and follow up on the actions agreed at the beginning of the next session

Coaching should create some kind of movement in you or your life *from the first session*. If you are just having a cosy chat or find that the sessions are meandering along in an unstructured manner, then you are not being coached.

On the other hand, it is also important that the coach is using methods to empower you in finding your own direction rather than simply telling you what to do. It may feel like a relief to have someone try to give you 'the answers' but it is far more empowering when they assist you in finding your own solutions. 'Non-directive' coaching will give you the inner skills to continue managing your life long after the coaching sessions have finished.

Always have an introductory session before signing up for a set of sessions with a new coach, however well recommended they are. Although it is not quite so important with coaching as it is with therapy, it can be worth shopping around before settling with a practitioner.

Singles Support Groups
It is easier to achieve most things with the support of others than to try achieving them in isolation. So, if you feel you would like the support of other women on this journey, you can always start your own support group for single women.

You may have a few single girlfriends who would be happy to get together regularly for meetings or you may want to put up an ad so you can meet with other like-minded women. You can make the group as formal or informal as you like, using whatever methods and resources feel appropriate to you and the group.

The important thing is that when you share the journey of self discovery with other women, you gain additional support, feedback and validation. *And the process becomes much more fun!*

References
[1]. John Gray, *Mars and Venus on a Date,* Vermillion London 2003

[2]. Laura Doyle, *The Surrendered Single,* Pocket Books 2006

[3]. As above

BOOKS

O is a symbol of the world, of oneness and unity. In different cultures it also means the "eye," symbolizing knowledge and insight. We aim to publish books that are accessible, constructive and that challenge accepted opinion, both that of academia and the "moral majority."

Our books are available in all good English language bookstores worldwide. If you don't see the book on the shelves ask the bookstore to order it for you, quoting the ISBN number and title. Alternatively you can order online (all major online retail sites carry our titles) or contact the distributor in the relevant country, listed on the copyright page.

See our website www.o-books.net for a full list of over 500 titles, growing by 100 a year.

And tune in to myspiritradio.com for our book review radio show, hosted by June-Elleni Laine, where you can listen to the authors discussing their books.